THE CLARITY CODE™

TRANSFORM COMPLEXITY INTO CLARITY

JEREMY SCOTT

AUTHORS NOTE

This book recounts real experiences and challenges I've encountered throughout my career. While all situations described are based on actual events, some dialogue, specific interactions, and scene details have been reconstructed, condensed, or dramatized for clarity and narrative flow. To protect privacy, names, identifying details, and specific organizational information have been changed or omitted. These stories focus on the systematic approaches for navigating complex challenges, not on critiquing any particular individuals or organizations.

TABLE OF CONTENTS

INTRODUCTION

WHEN EVERYTHING CHANGES

"Your stuck point isn't a dead end, it's a construction zone." ©

There's a moment in everyone's life when the path forward becomes invisible.

Not unclear. Not difficult. Invisible.

You're standing at what feels like a dead end, surrounded by walls you can't see over, under, or through. The strategies that worked before stop working. The harder you push, the more stuck you become. And the most maddening part? Everyone around you seems to have suggestions that sound logical but feel impossible to implement.

"Just network more." "Have you tried thinking positively?" "Maybe you need to work harder." "Perhaps it's time to lower your expectations."

This book is for you if you've found yourself in one of these invisible prisons, whether in your career, relationships, finances, health, or creative pursuits. Not because I have magical solutions, but because I discovered something powerful when trapped in my seemingly inescapable situation.

We live in an era where most people have access to more information, opportunities, and resources than any generation in history, yet millions feel more stuck than ever. The problem isn't a lack of options; it's the absence of systematic approaches for navigating situations where multiple variables intersect in confusing ways.

The CLARITY Code™ emerged from necessity, not theory. Every element has been tested under real pressure, refined through actual practice, and validated by helping others achieve tangible results. This mechanism isn't another motivational framework that tells you to 'think positive,' nor a collection of generic tactics. It's a comprehensive methodology for transforming complex challenges into manageable steps and breakthrough opportunities.

But here's what I need you to understand upfront: this book requires active engagement, not passive consumption. The frameworks only work when applied systematically to your actual situation. You'll need to answer difficult questions honestly, challenge assumptions you've held for years, and take strategic actions that might feel uncomfortable. The people who get results from this method are those who commit to working through each step thoroughly, not those hoping for quick fixes or magical insights.

To support your transformation journey, I've created The CLARITY Code™ Workbook, your hands-on companion with specific exercises, assessment tools, and structured reflection prompts that translate each principle into concrete progress on your actual situation. For those moments when you need deeper insights or encounter resistance, The CLARITY Navigator™ provides personalized coaching guidance and breakthrough perspectives. Together, these resources ensure you're not just reading about transformation but systematically experiencing it.

This experience taught me that gaining clarity isn't just about seeing your situation more clearly. It's about systematically transforming how you understand and navigate complex challenges when conventional approaches fail.

My Story: From Stuck to Strategic

Six months into what was supposed to be my dream job at a prestigious consulting firm, I found myself comprehensively stuck. Not just frustrated or challenged, truly, desperately stuck.

I was being systematically sabotaged by a colleague who saw me as a threat. The firm's culture made it nearly impossible to transfer projects. My industry expertise, which should have been an asset, had become a liability. And every attempt to improve the situation only seemed to make it worse.

Traditional advice wasn't just unhelpful; it revealed how poorly most people understand what it means to be truly stuck. Working harder didn't help when the game was rigged. Positive thinking didn't change organizational dynamics. And networking felt pointless when I didn't understand the real power structures at play.

The Birth of a Method

What saved me wasn't a sudden stroke of luck or a heroic intervention. It was developing a systematic approach to gaining clarity about my situation and using that clarity to create options where none seemed to exist.

Through months of trial, error, and eventual breakthrough, I unconsciously developed a seven-step process for navigating complex situations where conventional wisdom fails. At first, I thought it was just a personal survival strategy. But when I began helping others apply the same approach to their challenges (career transitions, relationship dilemmas, business obstacles, creative blocks), I realized I had stumbled onto something more universal.

The CLARITY Code™ isn't just another problem-solving framework. It's a comprehensive method for transforming how you see and respond to life's most challenging moments. It works because it addresses the real reason people stay stuck: not lack of options, but lack of clarity about their actual situation, genuine obstacles, and available resources.

Why CLARITY Changes Everything

Most approaches to getting unstuck focus on motivation, tactics, or mindset alone. But sustainable breakthroughs require something more comprehensive; a systematic way to:

- **C**onfront your current reality without denial or drama
- **L**ocate your desired destination with precision, not just vague aspirations
- **A**nalyze the real obstacles, not just the obvious ones
- **R**eframe limiting beliefs that constrain your options
- **I**dentify hidden resources you've been overlooking
- **T**ake strategic action that builds momentum
- **Y**ield sustainable momentum that compounds over time

Each element builds on the previous ones, creating a complete system for navigating from stuck to strategic, from trapped to transformed.

What You'll Discover

In this book, you'll learn:

- Why conventional approaches to problem-solving often make stuck situations worse
- How to see through the fog of confusion to identify what's really keeping you trapped
- The difference between surface obstacles and systemic barriers (and why it matters)
- How to transform limiting beliefs without pretending problems don't exist
- Why you probably have more resources than you realize, and how to recognize them
- The art of strategic action that creates compound results
- How to build momentum that sustains itself even when motivation fluctuates

You'll follow my journey from corporate nightmare to breakthrough insight, learning the method as it emerged through real-world pressure testing. You'll see how others have applied The CLARITY Code™ to challenges ranging from career transitions to relationship transformations, business breakthroughs, and creative resurrection.

Most importantly, you'll gain a systematic approach you can apply to any complex challenge for the rest of your life.

Your Journey Starts Now

Whatever situation has you feeling stuck right now (whether it's been days, months, or years in the making), you're about to discover that a breakthrough isn't about working harder or wanting it more. It's about gaining clarity that reveals options you couldn't see before.

The CLARITY Code™ works because it transforms not just your situation, but your entire approach to navigating complexity. It gives you a reliable method for facing challenges that don't respond to conventional solutions.

If you're ready to stop spinning your wheels and start making real progress, if you're tired of advice that sounds good but doesn't work in your specific situation, and if you want a systematic approach to creating breakthroughs in any area of life, let's begin.

Your journey from stuck to clarity starts with understanding how I discovered these principles in the crucible of my own impossible situation.

Welcome to The CLARITY Code™.

CHAPTER 1
WHEN EVERYTHING LOOKED PERFECT, BUT FELT EMPTY

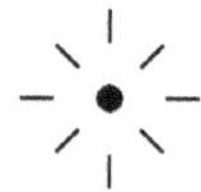

"I think we should probably table your suggestions for now and focus on approaches that are more aligned with what our tier-one clients are accustomed to seeing from consultants at this level."

That's what I heard sitting in a sterile conference room on my first day at a Big Four consulting firm, watching a colleague with zero healthcare experience systematically shut down every suggestion I made—suggestions based on more than a decade of industry knowledge. My stomach was sinking as I realized this wasn't about the work. This dynamic was about politics; I didn't even know I was playing.

I bet you're wondering how someone ends up in that situation. How do you go from feeling like you've finally made it to realizing you've been completely played? Sit back, and let me tell you exactly how it happens.

But first, let me share something crucial I learned through this experience: **The difference between being stuck and lacking clarity is the difference between spinning your wheels and finding traction.** When you're stuck, you know something's wrong but can't see the path forward.

When you gain clarity, the path doesn't just become visible; it becomes inevitable.

Most people think clarity is just about understanding your situation better. But true clarity is transformational. It's the systematic process of cutting through complexity, confusion, and competing priorities to see not just what is, but what's possible. It's what turns overwhelming challenges into manageable steps, and impossible situations into strategic opportunities.

That's what The CLARITY Code™ gave me when I was trapped in what felt like an impossible corporate nightmare. And what you're about to discover can work for any complex challenge where conventional approaches have failed.

Six months earlier, I was exactly where I thought I wanted to be. After three years of working full-time during the day and attending business school in the evenings, burning the midnight oil at a top-tier private university while managing student loans that would have crushed most people, I finally accomplished my goal of joining a Big Four consulting firm.

Let me be clear about what 'finally accomplished' actually meant. While some of my classmates could focus solely on their studies, I worked 50+ hour weeks to pay rent and living expenses. While others could afford test prep courses and application consultants, I studied for the GMAT using library books and free online resources. While others had family connections to smooth their path into consulting, I cold-called alums, attended every networking event, and practiced case studies until I could recite McKinsey frameworks in my sleep.

I mention this not for sympathy, but for context. When you've had to work systematically and strategically just to get a seat at the table, you develop different instincts about how systems really work versus how they're supposed to work. You learn to study the game being played, not just the rules written in the handbook. These instincts—born from necessity— would become crucial when I found myself trapped in what felt like an impossible situation.

The late nights in lecture halls after ten-hour workdays had been worth it. All that preparation and systematic effort had paid off. The student loans, the exhaustion, and the missed social events were all going to make sense.

After hours of case study prep and mock interviews with colleagues, I got my chance. A project manager interviewed me and led me through the entire process, and I was in.

But here's where it gets interesting. A few days before I was supposed to start, this same project manager, the one who had recruited me, sold me on the opportunity, painted this incredible picture of what my career could become, called me.

"Jeremy," he said, and I could hear the excitement in his voice. "I've got some news. I'm leaving the firm."

I felt my stomach drop, but he continued before I could respond.

"I just landed my dream job. Everything we discussed, all those opportunities I mentioned for your career path, I'm about to go live all that somewhere else."

Initially, I was supposed to work with him on his team. He had painted a picture that was absolutely compelling. He told me I'd be working with health systems, creating impactful strategies that would lead to growth through innovative marketing tactics. He described projects where I'd develop comprehensive approaches to help healthcare organizations expand their reach and improve their operations. The work would be strategic, meaningful, and directly aligned with the decade-plus of healthcare experience I brought to the table.

"You'll be traveling to client sites," he'd said during our interviews. "Getting face time with C-suite executives at major health systems. This isn't just consulting; you'll be helping shape the future of healthcare delivery."

He spoke about the mentorship I'd receive, the rapid career progression available to someone with my background, and how my industry expertise would make me invaluable to clients who were navigating complex operational challenges.

"Jeremy, with your healthcare background, you will stand out. These health systems need someone who understands their world from the inside. You're not just another consultant, you're someone who's lived their challenges."

It was everything I thought I wanted. Strategic work, travel, meaningful impact, career growth, and the prestige of working for a firm whose name opened doors everywhere.

And now, three days before I was supposed to start this dream job, the person who had sold me this vision was walking away to live it elsewhere.

But I was too committed to back out now. Too invested in the outcome. I was too eager to prove that all those late nights in business school had been worth it.

So I showed up for my first day, eyes front and head in the game, ready to dive into the world of healthcare consulting strategy.

That's when I met my new reality.

The reality hit me the moment I walked into the client site. After the standard orientation sessions that lasted a few days, I finally met the client-facing team, where the real work happened. I remember being introduced to the guy who would become the source of my corporate nightmare, and he didn't even turn around from his computer to meet me.

I stood awkwardly, hand half-extended for a handshake that would never come, while he continued typing.

"Jeremy Scott," I said to the back of his head. "Looking forward to working with you."

A grunt. Still no eye contact.

I remember thinking that was odd, but I let it slide. Everyone seemed busy, and I was the new guy. Maybe this was just the intensity of Big Four culture I'd heard so much about.

I should have trusted my instincts.

Within hours, the setup began. I started receiving emails with immediate deadlines and work that required access to client platforms I didn't have yet. The kind of access that takes time to get approved, especially at a sensitive healthcare organization that requires background checks and security clearances. This place was locked down, literally. Before I received my clearance and badge, I couldn't even go to the bathroom alone. I had to have someone escort me to the bathroom, like I might try to signal enemy agents via a series of strategic flushes.

But the emails kept coming.

"Jeremy, can you complete the analysis by the end of the day?"

"Just checking on the status of the client data review we discussed."

"Following up on the deliverables we need for tomorrow's meeting."

Each email was carefully crafted to create a paper trail, cc'ing the project manager and other team members. He was building a case that I wasn't delivering, even though he knew damn well I couldn't complete the work without system access, which he knew I didn't have.

That's when it became clear what was happening. He was setting me up to fail.

The conference room moment came later that week. We were sitting with the client, and I was finally able to contribute something meaningful. I'd noticed they were doing a lot of manual work in Word that could easily be automated in Excel—the kind of time-saving solution that would free up their team for more strategic work.

"Based on my experience automating similar processes," I said, addressing both my colleague and the client, "we could streamline these workflows significantly. If we transition some of these documents and automate certain sections, we could reduce the tedious workload and create more time for analysis."

The client's eyes lit up. "That sounds like exactly what we need. How quickly could we implement something like that?"

That's when he struck.

"I think we should probably table your suggestions for now and focus on approaches that are more aligned with what our tier-one clients are accustomed to seeing from consultants at this level."

The words hung in the air like a slap.

I watched the client's enthusiasm deflate. They nodded politely, deferring to his relationship and seniority. The project manager, who had been leaning forward with interest, sat back in his chair.

And I sat there, feeling my stomach drop as the whole picture became crystal clear.

This wasn't about the efficiency of my suggestion. This wasn't about client needs or best practices. This was about territory, insecurity, and corporate politics I hadn't even known I was playing.

He had no healthcare experience. I had over a decade. He was on the advisory side of the firm; I was consulting. My presence on his team offered him no benefit for his promotion goals, in fact, it threatened them. It was in his best interest to get me out of there so he could hire another consultant from the advisory side.

But here's what really got me: the client actually thought my idea was solid. I could see it in their faces before he shut it down. This wasn't about what was best for the client. This was about what was best for him.

Sitting in that sterile conference room, watching this guy systematically undermine every suggestion I made without logical reasoning, I realized something that would change everything about how I approached my career.

I found myself in a situation, dealing with corporate micro-aggressions and insecurities, and if I didn't figure out how to navigate it strategically, I was going to sink.

That's when I realized I was stuck.

The Immediate Aftermath

The rest of that meeting passed in a blur. I maintained professionalism, nodding at appropriate moments and taking notes like nothing had happened. But inside, my mind was racing.

As we filed out of the conference room, I caught a few of the other team members shaking their heads. One of them, someone I'd later learn had been watching this dynamic play out for weeks, gave me a look that said, "Welcome to the circus."

That evening, the walk back to the parking garage felt like a funeral march. The client site was about half a mile from the parking area, and since I didn't have client-site-specific parking yet, I had to make the trek to the distant lot with all the other newcomers and contractors.

I was walking alongside one of my female colleagues, Sarah, having a casual conversation about the day's meetings, when I heard footsteps approaching us. It was him, jogging slightly to reach us.

"Hey, Sarah," he called out, slightly out of breath and completely ignoring my presence. "Want a ride to your car?"

She glanced at me, then back at him. "That would be great, thanks."

They walked off together toward his vehicle, leaving me to continue my solitary march to the distant parking lot. I watched their car speed past me on the road, and for a moment, I thought that was it.

But here's what really stuck with me: their car slowed down about halfway to the lot and pulled over. They waited.

When I finally caught up, he rolled down the window with what I can only describe as a forced smile.

"Jeremy, you need a ride too?"

The way he asked, like it was an afterthought, like he was doing me this huge favor, told me everything I needed to know. Sarah had clearly made him ask. Left to his own devices, he would have driven right past me without a second thought.

I laughed internally and took the ride. But sitting in that backseat for those few awkward minutes, I knew I had trouble ahead. This wasn't just professional rivalry or healthy competition. This was personal, and it was going to get worse before it got better.

That night, I couldn't sleep. I kept replaying the conference room scene, the dismissive tone, the client's deflated response. I thought about all those late nights in business school, all the case studies and frameworks I'd memorized, all the networking events and career planning sessions.

None of it had prepared me for this.

I had expected competition. I had expected long hours, demanding clients, and complex problems to solve. What I hadn't expected was to be sabotaged by someone on my own team.

The worst part? I was starting to realize this was just the beginning.

That night, I sat in my car in my driveway for twenty minutes before going inside. I needed to process what had just happened before I faced my girlfriend—now my wife—and tried to explain why my dream job already felt like a nightmare.

When I finally walked through the front door, she took one look at my face and knew something was wrong.

"How was the first day?" she asked, settling onto the couch beside me.

"Different than expected," I said, telling her everything. The computer snub, the impossible deadlines, the conference room dismissal, the parking lot power play. All of it.

She listened without judgment, the way she always did, and then asked the question that would haunt me for the next six months: "So what are you going to do about it?"

That's when it hit me. I didn't know. For the first time in my professional life, I genuinely didn't know how to move forward.

I had always been the person who figured things out. When I wanted to advance my career, I went to business school. When I wanted to break into consulting, I networked and prepared until I landed the interview. When I faced challenges, I worked harder, got smarter, and found a way through.

But this was different. This wasn't about working harder or being more prepared. This was about navigating a game whose rules nobody had explained to me, where the person making the rules actively wanted me to fail.

I was an experienced hire, ready to take on any challenge in the world of consulting. I had a decade of healthcare experience, an advanced degree, and all the motivation in the world.

And I was completely, utterly stuck.

Not stuck like when you can't solve a problem and need to think harder. Stuck like when you're spinning your wheels in mud, applying more effort but going nowhere. Stuck like when you're playing a game where someone else keeps changing the rules, and you don't even know what the objective is supposed to be.

I had worked so hard to get to this point, sacrificed so much to earn this opportunity, and now I was trapped in a situation that felt designed to break me down rather than build me up.

That night, lying in bed staring at the ceiling, I realized something that would fundamentally change how I approached every challenge for the rest of my life:

Sometimes the problem isn't that you're not good enough. Sometimes the problem is that you're playing the wrong game entirely.

But I didn't know that yet. I knew I was stuck and had no idea how to get unstuck.

I didn't realize that over the next six months, this impossible situation would teach me everything I needed to know about clarity, strategy, and the difference between working hard and working smart.

I was about to get an education that no business school could provide. I was about to discover The CLARITY Code™.

CHAPTER 2
THE DOWNWARD SPIRAL

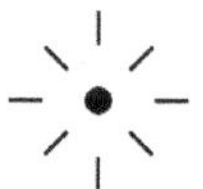

"Sometimes you have to hit rock bottom to realize you've been digging the wrong hole." ©

Six months. That's how long I stayed trapped in what I came to think of as corporate prison.

When people ask me about that period now, they often assume I was just being dramatic. "Why didn't you just quit?" they say. "Why didn't you transfer to another project? Why didn't you report him to HR?"

They don't understand that leaving wasn't as simple as walking away from a bad situation. This was a Big Four consulting firm with a particular culture and particular rules about how things worked. And rule number one was: when you're assigned to a project, you stay on that project until they're finished with you.

Period.

I learned this the hard way when I tried to do precisely what those well-meaning friends suggested. I went to one of the overall project leaders, a woman I thought would understand the impossible position I'd been put in, and explained my situation.

Her response was swift and brutal: "Jeremy, this is your first project at the firm. No matter what you're going through, you need to stay on this project and make it work. That's how we do things here."

She wasn't interested in hearing about the sabotage, the email traps, or the systematic undermining. She wasn't curious about why someone with my healthcare background wasn't being utilized effectively. She didn't care about the client's positive response to my suggestions or the obvious waste of resources happening under her watch.

She just didn't care a flying flip about me, who I was, what I was going through, or anything about the situation.

Walking out of that meeting, I felt completely deflated. It was like hitting a wall at full speed and realizing it would never move, no matter how hard you ran into it.

That's when the real spiral began. And that's when I started to understand something crucial: **without clarity about the system you're operating in, every action feels random and every outcome feels like luck, good or bad.**

I had been approaching this situation with complete opacity about how things really worked. I couldn't see the informal power structures, the unspoken rules, or the political dynamics that actually drove decisions. I was like someone trying to navigate a maze while blindfolded, wondering why every path seemed to lead to a dead end.

The Systematic Destruction

Over the following months, the guy I'd thought was just insecure and territorial revealed himself to be far more strategic in his sabotage than I'd initially realized.

He didn't just block my access to information; he actively spread misinformation about my performance. He'd have side conversations with the project manager about concerns with my work, conversations I wasn't invited to join. He'd raise questions about my approaches in team meetings, then pivot the discussion before I could respond.

The travel opportunities that the original project manager promised during my recruitment? Blocked. Every single one.

"We need someone with more project-specific experience for that client visit," he'd say, then send someone who'd been on the project for two weeks less than I had.

Critical information I needed to complete assignments would arrive in my inbox hours after deadlines had passed, with an apologetic note about how "things have been crazy" and he "forgot to loop me in earlier."

He tried to embarrass me in front of clients by asking me questions about aspects of the project he knew I hadn't been briefed on, then expressing "surprise" that I wasn't up to speed.

The most insidious part was how he did everything with a smile, always maintaining plausible deniability. To anyone watching casually, he appeared collaborative and supportive. The sabotage was surgical, precise, and completely deniable.

And it was working.

The Personal Toll

This wasn't just about work frustration. Spending forty-plus hours a week in an environment designed to make you fail starts affecting everything else.

I found myself falling into what I can only describe as a funk. For the first time in my professional life, I felt weak. Powerless. Like nothing I did to remediate the situation actually worked.

I've always been someone who figures things out. Give me a problem, and I'll find a solution. Put me in a challenging situation, and I'll adapt and overcome. But this was different. This was like being in quicksand; the harder I struggled using conventional approaches, the deeper I sank.

I'd come home exhausted not from the work, but from the constant vigilance required to protect myself. Every email had to be carefully crafted. Every meeting required strategic thinking about what wasn't being said. Every interaction felt like a chess match where my opponent knew all my moves before I made them.

My girlfriend, watched me go through this with a mixture of concern and frustration. She knew I had grit. She knew I was the person who always found a way. But she could also see that my usual approaches weren't working.

"You always figure it out," she'd tell me. "Wherever there's a will, there's a way, and you always find that way."

Her confidence in me was touching, but it also added pressure. Everyone believed I'd find a solution because I always had before. But what happens when your greatest strength, your ability to work hard and push through challenges, becomes irrelevant because you're facing a completely different type of problem?

I was learning, painfully and slowly, that **clarity isn't just about seeing what's happening, it's about understanding why it's happening and what forces are at play beneath the surface.**

Learning the Game

It took me about three months to realize I was approaching this all wrong.

I was treating this like a performance issue when it was actually a political issue. I tried to solve it with better work when the problem had nothing to do with work quality. I was operating under the assumption that merit and logic would eventually prevail when the system I was trapped in ran on entirely different principles.

The breakthrough came during casual conversations with other consultants. Not formal meetings or official channels, but coffee chats and hallway conversations where people let their guard down and told me what was really happening.

That's when I learned about the firm's coaching system, and more importantly, why mine wasn't working.

Every consultant was assigned a coach, supposedly someone who would advocate for you and provide guidance when you hit challenges. My coach lived several states away in an entirely different region. He was unhelpful, lackadaisical, and had zero influence within my business vertical.

"You need a coach who's actually here," one colleague told me during a frank conversation. "Someone in your business vertical who has clout. Your current coach might as well not exist."

That's when the lightbulb went off.

I wasn't just fighting one guy's insecurities and political maneuvering. I was trying to navigate a complex organizational system without understanding how that system actually worked. I'd been focusing on the symptoms, his behavior, the project dynamics, the immediate frustrations, when I should have been studying the underlying structure.

This was my first authentic taste of what would become The CLARITY Code™: **the systematic process of cutting through surface-level confusion to see the deeper patterns and structures that actually determine outcomes.**

The Strategic Shift

Once I understood this, everything changed.

I stopped trying to prove myself to someone who had already decided I was a threat. I stopped expecting logic and merit to solve problems that were fundamentally about power and influence. And I started doing homework.

I researched who had clout in my business vertical. I identified the people my project manager looked up to and respected. I studied the informal hierarchy that really drove decisions, not just the organizational chart that existed on paper.

Then I started networking. Not random networking, but strategic relationship building with specific people who could potentially help me navigate the system I was trapped in.

This wasn't about complaining or asking for rescue. It was about understanding the game that was actually being played and finding ways to play it more effectively.

I had multiple one-on-ones with consultants and senior leaders, asking questions about career development and getting their perspectives on success at the firm. Gradually, I pieced together the real power dynamics and influence patterns within our business vertical.

That's when I identified my target: a high-level practitioner who had the kind of clout that could actually move mountains. Someone, my project manager, not only respected but whose opinion could literally make or break his promotion prospects.

I set up a meeting.

This was the beginning of my education in what I now call "Confronting your current reality," the C in The CLARITY Code™. It wasn't enough to acknowledge that I was in a difficult situation. I had to see clearly and completely how the system around me actually functioned, not how I wished it functioned or how it was supposed to function according to the employee handbook.

The Setup

The beauty of this firm was that they strongly encouraged internal networking. You were expected to build relationships with senior leaders across the organization. So when I reached out to this leader asking for time to discuss career development and learn from his experience, it was perfectly normal and appropriate.

I didn't lead with my problems. I led with genuine curiosity about his career path and perspectives on the industry. I asked thoughtful questions about his approach to client relationships and what he'd learned about succeeding in consulting.

But naturally, as the conversation evolved, he asked about my experience at the firm so far. What were the pros and cons? How was I finding the culture? What challenges was I facing?

That's when I mentioned, almost in passing, how difficult it was having a coach who lived several states away. I'd appreciate having someone local who could provide more regular guidance and support.

It wasn't a complaint. It was an observation about a structural challenge that any reasonable person could understand.

We had several of these conversations over a few weeks. I was genuinely building a relationship, not just working an angle. But I was also planting seeds and gathering intelligence about how things really worked at this level of the organization.

Eventually, during one of these conversations, I asked the question that would change everything:

"Would you consider taking me on as one of your coaching clients? I know you have a full roster, but I'd really value having someone local who understands our business vertical."

He thought about it for a moment, then smiled.

"Actually, one of my mentees just left the firm, so I do have an opening. Let me think about it."

A week later, I was officially his coaching client.

That's when I dropped the seed with my project manager during one of our routine check-ins.

"By the way," I mentioned casually, "I've switched coaches. I'm working with Jason now."

I watched his eyes get big.

"Yes," I said, trying to look completely innocent. "He's been incredibly helpful so far."

The change in dynamics was immediate and unmistakable.

Suddenly, my project manager was much more amenable to discussions about my career development and potential transitions to other projects. The conversation about me rolling off the engagement, which had been impossible for months, became not just possible, but actively supported.

Six months after starting what I thought would be my dream job, I finally had my exit strategy.

But more importantly, I had learned something that would change how I approached every complex situation for the rest of my life: **No situation is truly inescapable when you understand the system you're operating within.**

The question isn't whether you can get clarity about your situation. The question is whether you're willing to learn the rules of the game that's actually being played.

I was about to find out just how powerful that lesson could be.

CHAPTER 3
THE AWAKENING

"Your worst situation often teaches you your most valuable skills." ©

Liberation felt like stepping out of a cage I didn't even know I was in.

Walking out of that client site for the final time, with a bookbag full of personal items in hand, I should have felt relief. And I did. But more than that, I felt something I hadn't experienced in months: power.

Not the kind of power that comes from a title or a corner office, but the quiet confidence that comes from understanding how things really work. I had learned to see the invisible forces that shape every organization, every relationship, every complex situation where people feel trapped.

I had learned to gain clarity about a game I didn't even know existed six months earlier.

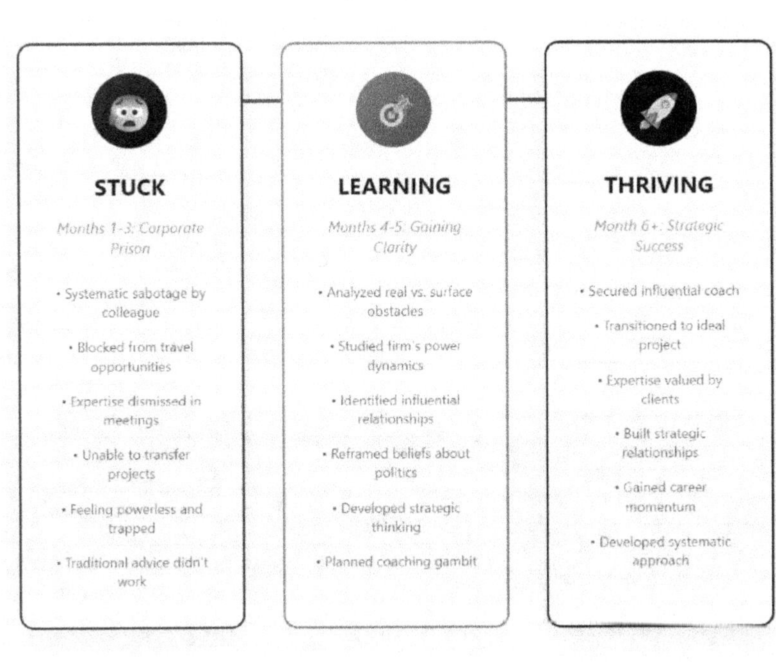

But here's what's interesting: the real awakening didn't happen when I walked out of that toxic project. It happened in the following weeks, when I started reflecting on what I'd accomplished.

What I discovered would become the foundation of The CLARITY Code™.

The Clarity Code™ in Action

The Problem Wasn't Performance

The real obstacle was organizational politics and power dynamics, not work quality or competence.

Systems Thinking Worked

Understanding how the firm actually operated revealed strategic opportunities invisible to surface-level analysis.

Strategic Action Created Leverage

The coaching gambit addressed multiple obstacles simultaneously while demonstrating strategic thinking.

Capabilities Transferred

The methodology developed for this crisis became applicable to any complex organizational challenge.

The Fundamental Insight

"Sometimes the problem isn't that you're not good enough. Sometimes the problem is that you're playing the wrong game entirely. The CLARITY Code™ teaches you to see the game that's actually being played and develop strategies that work within that reality."

The Debrief

My new coach, the one with actual clout, scheduled a debrief session about a week after my transition. We met at a coffee shop downtown, away from the office politics and corporate theater.

"So," he said, stirring his coffee thoughtfully, "walk me through how you handled that situation. From a strategic perspective."

It was the first time anyone had asked me to analyze what I'd done rather than just sympathize with what had happened to me. And as I walked through my approach step by step, I realized something remarkable:

I had unconsciously developed a systematic method for gaining clarity in complex situations.

"First," I explained, "I had to get honest about where I really was. Not where I wanted to be or where I thought I should be, but the actual reality of my situation."

He nodded. "That's harder than it sounds. Most people spend so much energy managing their story that they lose sight of the facts."

"Exactly. I spent the first few months thinking this was about my performance or my approach to the work. I had to confront the fact that it was actually about politics and power dynamics I didn't understand."

"Then what?"

"Then I had to get clear about what I actually wanted. Not just 'get out of this situation,' but specifically what a good outcome would look like. I realized I wanted to transition to a different project without burning bridges or damaging my reputation at the firm."

"Smart. Vague goals create vague results. What else?"

"I had to analyze the real obstacles. The obvious obstacle was this guy's behavior, but the real obstacle was the system that kept me trapped despite his behavior. The coaching structure, the project assignment process, the informal power networks I didn't understand."

My coach leaned back in his chair, smiling slightly. "Go on."

"That's when I realized I had been thinking about this all wrong. Instead of trying to change the situation or prove this guy wrong, I needed to work within the system as it actually existed. I had to reframe my beliefs about what was possible and how things got done."

"And then?"

"Then I took inventory of what resources I actually had. I'd been so focused on what I lacked, influence, seniority, insider knowledge, that I missed what I did have. I could network. I could build relationships. I had legitimate reasons to connect with senior people."

"The coaching switch," he said. "That was brilliant, by the way."

"Thanks. But the key wasn't just getting a new coach. It was getting the right coach. Someone whose opinion mattered to the people whose decisions affected me."

"And then?"

"Then I took strategic action and executed it systematically. Not all at once, but building relationships and gathering intelligence step by step until I had the leverage I needed."

"And the final piece?"

"Maintaining momentum. Making sure the change stuck and I didn't slide back into the same pattern somewhere else."

We sat in silence for a moment. Then my coach said something that would stick with me for years:

"Jeremy, do you realize you just described a methodology that could work in almost any complex situation where someone feels stuck?"

I hadn't realized it. But he was right.

The Pattern Recognition

Over the following weeks, I found myself thinking about that conversation constantly. Had I really developed a systematic approach to gaining clarity? Was it something that could be replicated?

I started paying attention to how I approached other challenges at work and in my personal life. I noticed that I naturally seemed to follow a similar pattern:

Confront the current reality honestly. Locate the desired destination precisely. Analyze the real obstacles. Reframe limiting beliefs about what was possible. Identify available resources. Take strategic action. Yield sustainable momentum.

It wasn't just about the consulting situation. It was how I approached everything.

When friends came to me with problems—which happened more often than I'd realized—I unconsciously guided them through a similar process. I'd help them get clear about what was really happening, what they actually wanted, and what resources they already had available to them.

I started noticing something else: I was the person people came to when they felt stuck.

Not for technical advice or specific expertise, but for that moment when they couldn't see a way forward and needed someone to help them think through their situation differently.

My serial entrepreneur friend who always needed help with financial negotiations and pricing strategies. Colleagues who were navigating difficult office politics. Family members trying to make major life decisions.

The pattern was consistent: they'd come to me when they felt trapped or overwhelmed, and I'd help them see possibilities they couldn't see on their own.

This was the birth of what I now recognize as The CLARITY Code™—a systematic approach to transforming complexity into clarity, confusion into direction, and obstacles into opportunities.

The Broader Application

About two months into my new project, which was everything the original had promised to be, I had a conversation that would prove to be a turning point.

I was having coffee with a colleague from a different business unit, someone I'd met during the networking phase of my escape strategy. We were catching up on our respective projects when he mentioned that he was struggling with his own situation.

"I'm in this weird spot," he said. "I love the work, but I feel like I'm invisible. My manager barely acknowledges my contributions, and I can't figure out how to get on more high-visibility projects."

Without thinking, I started asking questions. What specifically did he want to achieve? What had he already tried? Who were the decision-makers for project assignments? What relationships did he have that he might be underutilizing?

As we talked through his situation, I watched him shift from feeling helpless to feeling strategic. By the end of our conversation, he had a clear plan for building relationships with key project leaders and positioning himself for better opportunities.

"Man," he said as we were wrapping up, "you should do this professionally. You have a real gift for helping people see their way out of complex situations."

It was the first time anyone had suggested that my approach to gaining clarity could be something more than just personal problem-solving.

The Ripple Effect

I was beginning to understand that my experience in that toxic consulting project had taught me something more valuable than how to navigate corporate politics.

It had taught me how to think systematically about any situation where someone feels trapped, confused, or unable to move forward.

The specific tactics I'd used, the networking, the coaching switch, the strategic relationship building, those were just tools. The real breakthrough was the underlying framework: the recognition that feeling stuck is usually about not understanding the system you're operating within, and that there's always a way forward when you learn to see that system clearly.

This realization was reinforced every time someone came to me for advice. The details were always different: career challenges, relationship issues, business decisions, creative blocks, but the underlying pattern was remarkably consistent.

People gained clarity when they:

- Were honest about their current reality
- Were clear about what they actually wanted
- Focused on real obstacles while understanding systemic ones
- Operated from empowering beliefs about what was possible
- Leveraged resources they already had access to
- Took a strategic approach to moving forward
- Built sustainable momentum once they started making progress

And they remained stuck when they struggled with any of these areas systematically.

The Emerging Methodology

I didn't set out to create a method. It just emerged from repeatedly helping people think through their stuck points in a more structured way.

I'd find myself saying things like:

"Let's start by getting really clear about where you are right now, without any sugar-coating or wishful thinking."

"Now, what would success actually look like in this situation? Not what you think you should want, but what you actually want."

"Okay, what's really preventing that from happening? And I mean really— not just the obvious stuff, but the deeper systemic issues."

"What assumptions are you making about this situation that might not be true?"

"What do you already have access to that you might be overlooking?"

"If you were going to solve this strategically rather than just hoping for the best, what would your plan look like?"

"How will you make sure this change sticks once you implement it?"

The more I used this approach, the more consistently it seemed to work. Not just for big career crises like mine but for smaller daily challenges, relationship issues, creative projects, health goals, and anywhere someone felt stuck or unable to move forward.

I was beginning to suspect that I had stumbled onto something bigger than just a personal problem-solving toolkit.

The more I used this approach, the more consistently it seemed to work. Not just for big career crises like mine, but for smaller daily challenges, relationship issues, creative projects, health goals, and anywhere someone felt stuck or unable to move forward.

But I wasn't ready to call it a "method" or think about it as something formal. It just felt like how I naturally approached problems. I'd always been the person people came to for advice, and now I was starting to understand why.

I was still at the consulting firm, still navigating the complexities of corporate life, but with a completely different perspective. I had learned something fundamental about how systems work and why people get stuck in them. More importantly, I had learned that there was always a way forward when you understood the game that was actually being played.

But I was curious about something else. If this approach to gaining clarity was so effective, and if people naturally came to me for this kind of help, what did that say about my actual talents and strengths?

February was approaching, my birthday month, and I was in a reflective mood about what I'd accomplished over the past year and where I wanted to go next. The consulting experience had been traumatic, but it had also been transformative. I felt like I'd discovered something important about myself, but I couldn't quite put my finger on what it was.

That's when I decided to do something I'd never done: systematically analyze my own talents and abilities. Not what my resume said I was good at, not what I'd been trained to do, but what I naturally excelled at and what people actually came to me for.

I had no idea that this simple exercise would reveal the foundation of everything that would follow, and crystallize what would become The CLARITY Code™.

CHAPTER 4
DECONSTRUCTING THE SYSTEM

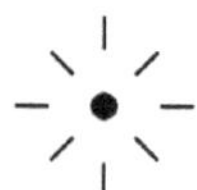

"Your natural talents aren't accidents, they're instructions." ©

I remember the date because I was inching closer to my birthday and sitting at my kitchen table asking myself a question that would change everything: "What am I actually good at?"

It sounds like such a simple question, but I'd never approached it systematically. I'd spent years climbing ladders, checking boxes, and pursuing what I thought success should look like. But after navigating that toxic consulting situation and emerging with new insights about how complex systems really work, I realized I needed to understand what I naturally did well—not what my resume said I should be good at.

I opened a fresh Excel spreadsheet and created simple column headers across the top:

Talent/Skill | Is This Burdensome to Me? | How Much Effort Does This Require? | Do People Ask Me For Help With This?

Then I started writing. Line by line, I documented everything I could think of that came naturally to me. Not just professional skills, but patterns I'd noticed about how I approached problems, what people asked me for help with, and what energized me versus what drained me.

What I was about to discover would become the foundation of The CLARITY Code™.

The Talent Analysis Framework

Part 1: The Systematic Analysis Process

Skills & Talents Assessment Methodology

"I opened a fresh Excel spreadsheet and created simple column headers across the top. Then I started writing—line by line, documenting everything I could think of that came naturally to me."

Talent/Skill	Is This Burdensome?	Effort Required	People Ask for Help?	Natural Talent Score
Helping people see possibilities	Low	Low	High	★★★
Strategic thinking & planning	Low	Medium	High	★★★
Breaking down complex problems	Low	Low	High	★★★
Financial analysis	Medium	Medium	Medium	★★
Connecting people with resources	Low	Low	High	★★★
Project management	Medium	Medium	Low	★★
Reframing perspectives	Low	Low	High	★★★
Technical writing	High	High	Low	★
Motivating people to take action	Low	Medium	High	★★★
Data visualization	High	High	Low	★

The items where I scored highest across all categories—things people frequently asked for help with, that didn't feel burdensome, that required minimal effort but had high value—all had something in common.

The List

Some of the entries were obvious professional skills: financial analysis, strategic thinking, project management. But as I kept writing, other patterns emerged:

- Thinking outside the box and finding creative solutions
- Reviewing complex situations and determining if there was a different use-case or approach
- Reading people and understanding their motivations
- Getting reactions out of people and motivating them to take action
- Figuring out loopholes and alternative methods for achieving desired outcomes
- Helping people feel better about themselves and their capabilities
- Talking people into doing things they're unsure about or think might be impossible
- Wordsmithing and communicating complex ideas clearly
- Connecting people with others who could help them
- Seeing potential in situations where others see only problems

The Pattern Recognition

As I filled in the columns, something remarkable started to emerge. The items where I scored highest across all categories were things people frequently asked for help with, that didn't feel burdensome to me, that required minimal effort but had high value; all had something in common.

They were all variations on the same theme: helping people transform complexity into clarity.

The Talent Analysis Framework

Part 2A: The Pattern Discovery

The Pattern That Changed Everything

"They were all variations on the same theme: helping people transform complexity into clarity. I had always thought of this as just being a good friend or colleague. But when I saw it laid out systematically, I realized it was actually a specific talent."

What the Data Revealed

→ Highest scores clustered around helping others gain clarity

→ Natural talents felt "effortless" but were highly valued by others

→ People consistently sought help with stuck situations

→ Pattern revealed unconscious competence in clarity creation

→ What felt "normal" was actually exceptional capability

The Universal Pattern

→ Friends asking for advice on career decisions

→ Colleagues seeking guidance on office politics

→ Family members trying to figure out life situations

→ People coming when they felt trapped or confused

→ Helping people see possibilities they couldn't see alone

When I looked at the "Do People Ask Me For Help With This?" column, the clearest pattern was people coming to me when they felt trapped, confused, or unable to see a path forward. Friends asking for advice on career decisions. Colleagues seeking guidance on navigating office politics. Family members trying to figure out complex life situations.

I had always thought of this as just being a good friend or colleague. But when I saw it laid out systematically, I realized it was actually a specific talent: the ability to help people see possibilities they couldn't see on their own.

This was the moment I first understood what would become The CLARITY Code™: a systematic approach to cutting through confusion and complexity to reveal the path forward.

The Deeper Analysis

I sent this spreadsheet to a few trusted colleagues and mentors, asking for their perspective. Did these patterns match what they observed about my natural abilities? Were there things I was missing or overemphasizing?

The feedback was consistent and enlightening.

"You're the person people call when they feel stuck and don't know what to do next," one colleague wrote back. "You have this ability to ask the right questions that help people figure out their own solutions."

Another responded: "I've never thought about it before, but you're right, whenever I have a complex situation that feels impossible, you're one of the first people I think to reach out to. You help people see options they didn't know existed."

The most insightful feedback came from a mentor who had watched me navigate various challenges over the years: "What you do isn't just problem-solving. You help people change how they think about their problems. That's why your solutions often seem obvious in hindsight but weren't visible to the person beforehand."

The Revelation

Sitting there with my completed spreadsheet and the feedback from people who knew me well, I had a moment of clarity that felt almost like a physical shift.

I wasn't just good at gaining clarity for myself. I was naturally talented at helping others transform their confusion into clarity.

This wasn't random advice-giving or casual problem-solving. There was a consistent pattern to how I approached these situations, and there were consistent results. People didn't just feel better after talking with me—they had specific next steps and a clearer sense of what was possible.

I reflected on my recent consulting experience and realized that what I'd developed there wasn't just a personal survival strategy. It was a systematic approach to navigating complex situations that could be applied much more broadly.

The Talent Analysis Framework

Part 2B: Application & Breakthrough

Questions for Your Own Analysis

Use these breakthrough questions to discover your own natural talents and systematic approaches:

What do people regularly ask for my help with?

What feels easy to me but difficult for others?

Where do I naturally add value without effort?

What patterns exist across different contexts?

When do I feel most like myself?

What activities make me lose track of time?

The Life-Changing Realization

"I wasn't just good at solving my own problems—I had a natural, systematic talent for helping others transform confusion into clarity. What I thought was just being helpful was actually a repeatable methodology that could be developed and shared with people who needed exactly this kind of systematic approach."

Understanding the Universal Problem

The more I reflected on this, the more I understood something fundamental about why people get stuck.

Most people get stuck not because they lack capabilities or resources, but because they can't see the system they're operating within clearly enough to navigate it effectively.

Think about my consulting situation. I had all the technical skills needed to succeed. I had healthcare expertise, analytical capabilities, and work ethic. But I was stuck because I didn't understand the political and social systems that actually determined success in that environment.

This pattern showed up everywhere:

- People stuck in careers they'd outgrown because they couldn't see alternative paths or didn't understand how career transitions actually work

- Entrepreneurs are stuck in business plateaus because they are focused on tactics instead of understanding the systemic changes needed for growth

- Individuals are stuck in relationship patterns because they couldn't see how their own behavior was contributing to the dynamics they wanted to change

- Creative people get stuck in blocks because they are fighting their natural process instead of working with it

In every case, being stuck wasn't about lacking ability or resources. It was about not clearly seeing the whole picture to identify leverage points for change.

This insight would become the core philosophy of The CLARITY Code™: that breakthrough happens not through harder effort, but through clearer seeing.

The Systematic Approach

I was starting to understand that my natural approach to helping people gain clarity followed a consistent pattern, whether conscious of it or not.

I'd start by helping them get really honest about their current situation—not just the surface-level frustrations, but the deeper dynamics at play.

Then I'd help them get clear about what they actually wanted, not what they thought they should want or what seemed most reasonable.

I'd guide them to identify the real obstacles, which were often different from the obvious ones they'd been focused on.

I'd challenge assumptions and limiting beliefs that were constraining their thinking about what was possible.

I'd help them recognize resources and capabilities they already had but weren't fully utilizing.

We'd develop a strategic plan that worked with the systems and dynamics involved rather than against them.

And I'd help them think through how to maintain momentum and avoid sliding back into old patterns.

This was the birth of what would become the C.L.A.R.I.T.Y. framework:

C - Confront your current reality **L** - Locate your desired destination **A** - Analyze the real obstacles **R** - Reframe limiting beliefs **I** - Identify hidden resources **T** - Take strategic action **Y** - Yield sustainable momentum

The Business Insight

Looking at my spreadsheet analysis, one thing became crystal clear: this talent I had for helping people transform complexity into clarity was valuable, it came naturally to me, and there was consistent demand for it.

But I'd never thought about it as something I could build a business around. It was just something I did for friends and colleagues when they needed help.

What if it could be more than that?

I wasn't ready to act on that question yet. I was still building my consulting career and had plenty to focus on at work. But the seed was planted.

I had identified something I was naturally good at, that people valued, and that addressed a universal human challenge. I had unconsciously developed a systematic approach to helping people navigate complex situations and create forward momentum.

Most importantly, I had started to understand that my consulting experience, as difficult as it had been, had actually given me something valuable: a deep understanding of how systems work and why people get stuck in them.

I just didn't know yet how powerful that understanding could be when applied intentionally and systematically.

That realization would come later, when I unconsciously applied this approach to help the person closest to me navigate her career crisis.

But first, I had to continue developing my understanding of what I was actually doing when I helped people gain clarity. I needed to reverse-engineer my natural process so I could teach it to others.

That journey of discovery was just beginning.

CHAPTER 5
THE LABORATORY OF REAL LIFE

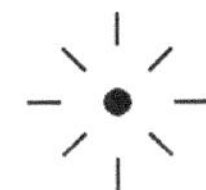

"Your insights truly take flight when they lift the burdens from another's shoulders." ©

The spreadsheet had revealed the pattern, but patterns mean nothing without proof. Over the months that followed my self-analysis, I found myself paying closer attention to the moments when people came to me for help. I discovered that I wasn't just naturally good at helping people gain clarity, I was unconsciously applying a systematic approach every single time.

Two situations in particular would prove to be perfect laboratories for understanding what I was actually doing when I helped people navigate complex challenges and transform confusion into clarity.

The Contract Negotiation

My friend Marcus had always been a dreamer with execution skills, a rare combination. He was a multilingual serial entrepreneur and had a natural ability to talk his way into opportunities that seemed impossible for others. But he had one consistent blind spot: the financial side of business.

When he called me one afternoon, his excitement was palpable but tinged with anxiety.

"Jeremy, I think I've got something big here, but I need your brain on the numbers."

Marcus had been building a business focused on language training and translation services, leveraging his ability to speak multiple languages fluently. Through his natural networking and relationship-building skills, he'd managed to get into serious negotiations with a state government agency. They needed someone to develop language training programs and help one of their departments communicate effectively with residents who spoke foreign languages.

"This could be life-changing," he said, "but I'm completely stuck on how to price this thing. I don't want to lowball myself, but I also don't want to price myself out of the opportunity. And honestly, I don't even know how government contracts work."

I could hear the frustration in his voice. Here was someone who had successfully navigated the complex process of getting a government agency interested in his services—no small feat—but he felt powerless when it came to the financial negotiation.

Marcus was experiencing a classic clarity crisis: he could see his destination (winning the contract), but couldn't see the path to get there because the system he was operating in was opaque to him.

"Walk me through what you know so far," I said.

As he described the situation, I naturally fell into what I now recognize as The CLARITY Code™ approach, though I wasn't conscious of it at the time.

First, I helped him **confront his current reality**. What exactly were they asking for? What was the scope of work? What timeline were they working with? How mission-critical was this service to their department?

"They need this badly," Marcus said. "The department is struggling to serve a growing population of non-English speakers, and it's becoming a real problem for them."

"Good. That's leverage. What else do you know about their situation?"

Then I guided him toward **locating his desired destination** with precision. What would a good outcome look like? Not just any contract, but the right contract at the right price that set him up for long-term success.

"I want to win this," he said, "but I also want to establish myself as the go-to expert for this type of work. This feels like it could open doors to similar opportunities."

"Perfect. So we're not just pricing a one-time project. We're pricing the foundation of a new business vertical for you."

Next came **analyzing the real obstacles**. What was really preventing him from confidently pricing this opportunity?

The obvious obstacle was lack of information about market rates and government contracting. But as we talked, the deeper obstacle emerged: he didn't fully understand the value he was providing or how to quantify it.

"You're not just teaching language skills," I told him. "You're solving a operational problem that's impacting their ability to serve constituents. That's worth a lot more than hourly language instruction."

That's when we got to work on **reframing his limiting thinking** about the situation.

"Here's what we're going to do," I said. "We're going to research this like we're preparing for a business school case study."

I walked him through a systematic research approach:

First, we'd look at market rates for similar services. What were other consultants charging for language training development? What did corporate language services cost?

Second, we'd research the transparency portals that most state and local governments maintain. These show budgets, vendor payments, and contract awards. We could see what they'd paid for similar services in the past.

Third, we'd assess the mission-critical nature of his work. How much was their current communication problem costing them? What was the risk of not solving it?

Fourth, we'd evaluate the innovative aspect of his approach. Was he bringing something unique that justified premium pricing?

Over the next week, Marcus did the research while I helped him **identify hidden resources** he hadn't been leveraging. The transparency portal data was particularly revealing; they had a budget allocated for this type of work, and their previous contracts suggested they understood the value of professional services.

When it came time to **take strategic action**, we built his pricing strategy around multiple factors:

- Market rates for comparable work

- The strategic value of solving their communication challenges

- His unique bilingual expertise and cultural understanding

- The innovation of his training approach

- The long-term relationship potential

"Don't just submit a price," I advised. "Submit a value proposition that shows exactly why your approach is worth the investment."

Marcus went into that final negotiation with complete confidence. He understood what to charge and why he was worth it. He could articulate the value he was providing in terms that mattered to them.

Two months later, he called with the news: he'd won the contract at the price point we'd developed. More importantly, the client had been impressed with his strategic approach to the proposal and was already talking about additional projects.

Marcus had transformed confusion into clarity by systematically understanding the system he was operating within, rather than just hoping for the best.

The Career Pivot

The second situation was different but followed a remarkably similar pattern.

My friend David had always been successful by conventional measures. He'd completed a policy degree, landed a good job at a major non-profit in Washington, D.C., and was building a respectable career in his field. But something was missing.

We were at a networking happy hour, one of those events David was famous for organizing, when he pulled me aside.

"I need to ask you something," he said, looking unusually serious. "Do you ever feel like you're successful at something that doesn't actually fulfill you?"

I looked around at the networking event he'd put together. It was a perfectly executed good venue, an interesting mix of people, and meaningful conversations happening everywhere. David had a gift for bringing people together and creating experiences that benefited everyone involved.

"Tell me more," I said.

"I'm good at policy work," he explained. "I understand the issues, I can write reports, I can navigate the political dynamics. But when I'm planning events like this, or figuring out how to get funding for a conference, or connecting people who should know each other, that's when I feel alive. That's when time disappears."

He described feeling stuck between what he was trained to do and what energized him. He'd invested years in building policy expertise, but his passion clearly lay elsewhere.

As we talked, I guided him through the same systematic process I'd used with Marcus, though I still wasn't conscious of the pattern.

First, we **confronted his current reality**. He was successful in policy but unfulfilled. He was naturally talented at marketing, event planning, and relationship building, but had never considered these as career paths.

"David," I said, "you're a master people connector. You have a natural gift for marketing strategy. You create experiences that bring out the best in people and generate real value for everyone involved."

I watched his face change as I described what I observed about his natural talents. It was like I was giving him permission to see himself differently.

"But I don't have a business background," he said. "I wouldn't even know where to start."

That's where we worked on **reframing his limiting beliefs** about what was possible.

"You know what people in marketing strategy roles actually do?" I asked. "They identify audiences, create experiences, products, and services that resonate or create value with those audiences, and build systems for connecting people with that value. Look around this room—that's exactly what you're doing right now."

We pulled out a napkin and started **analyzing his real obstacles** by sketching a decision tree. What were his options for transitioning into a marketing strategy? He could try to pivot within his current organization, look for entry-level roles at other companies, or get additional training to bridge the gap.

"If you want to make this transition," I said, "you probably need an MBA. Not because you need to learn how to market, you already know that intuitively, but because you need the credential and the network that comes with it."

"But MBA programs are expensive, and I already have student loans."

"So we research programs that offer scholarships or fellowships. There are programs specifically designed for people with non-business backgrounds who want to pivot."

Now we were **identifying hidden resources** he hadn't recognized. Over the following weeks, David and I researched MBA programs with fellowship opportunities. We found several that offered full scholarships for candidates who met specific criteria and were accepted to top business schools.

David threw himself into **taking strategic action** with the same energy he brought to event planning. He studied for the GMAT, crafted essays that highlighted his unique background, and networked with alumni and admissions staff.

When the acceptance letters came, he had multiple options, including a fellowship at one of the top business schools in the country.

Fast forward to today: David has held multiple brand marketing and strategy roles at reputable organizations. He's thriving in his career, using his natural talents for connection and experience creation in ways that feel both professionally rewarding and personally fulfilling. He successfully **yielded sustainable momentum** by building on his breakthrough rather than treating it as a one-time event.

The Pattern Emerges

Reflecting on these two very different situations, I started to see the consistent approach I was unconsciously applying:

1. **Confront the current reality** - Both Marcus and David had to acknowledge the gap between where they were and where they wanted to be.

2. **Locate the desired destination** - Marcus wanted to win the contract and establish himself as an expert; David wanted to align his career with his natural talents.

3. **Analyze the real obstacles** - For Marcus, it was a lack of pricing knowledge and confidence in his value; for David, it was limiting beliefs about his qualifications and being unclear about the path forward.

4. **Reframe limiting thinking** - Marcus learned to see himself as solving strategic problems, not just teaching languages; David learned to see his natural talents as valuable business skills.

5. **Identify hidden resources** - Marcus had his language skills and networking ability; David had his event planning success and relationship-building gifts.

6. **Take strategic action plans** - Both situations required research, preparation, and systematic execution.

7. **Yield sustainable momentum** - Both friends followed through completely and built on their initial success.

In both cases, the people didn't lack capability or resources. They were stuck because they couldn't see their situations clearly enough to navigate them strategically.

Marcus had the skills to deliver excellent language training, but he couldn't see how to value and price his expertise appropriately. David had natural marketing talents but couldn't see how to transition them into a career path.

What I provided wasn't magical insight or special expertise. I helped them see their situations from a different perspective and think through their challenges systematically.

This was the moment I realized I had unconsciously developed what would become The CLARITY Code™: a systematic methodology for transforming complexity into clarity, confusion into direction, and obstacles into opportunities.

But here's what was becoming clear: this wasn't just good friendship or casual advice-giving. A consistent methodology emerged in how I approached these situations.

I just didn't know yet how powerful that methodology could be when applied consciously and systematically.

That realization was still to come.

CHAPTER 6
THE MENTOR'S CHALLENGE

"You need to formalize that method and run with it." ©

Those eight words, spoken over coffee on a Tuesday morning, would change the trajectory of my life.

I was catching up with a colleague from my professional networking organization, someone I respected for his entrepreneurial mindset and natural coaching ability. He was a community leader, the kind of person who seemed to help others see possibilities they'd been missing effortlessly.

Which is why what happened next was so unexpected.

The Setup

We'd scheduled our usual quarterly coffee chat, one of those informal check-ins that keep professional relationships warm without any specific agenda. I was looking forward to hearing about his latest ventures and getting his perspective on some of the projects I was working on.

The conversation started typically enough. We talked about our careers, industry trends, and mutual connections. But naturally, he brought up entrepreneurial topics focused on goals, commercializing ideas, and skills. He then asked about my personal life and if I had given more thought to entrepreneurship or a side hustle. He then discussed how a lot of small business ideas came out of skillsets acquired, passions, or minor interests that people stumbled across or held. We started talking about gifts I have that I wasn't taking full advantage of, so I told him about Marcus's government contract success, David's MBA journey, and my knack for helping people transform complexity into clarity.

"That's amazing," he said. "You helped both of them navigate really complex situations. Walk me through how you approached those."

I started describing the process almost casually, how I'd helped Marcus research market rates, understand his value proposition, and guided David to see his natural marketing talents and develop a transition strategy.

But as I talked, I noticed his expression changing. He was leaning forward, asking more detailed questions, taking notes on his phone.

"Hold on," he said, interrupting my description of David's decision tree. "This isn't just friendly advice you're giving people. This is a systematic approach to helping people solve complex problems."

The Recognition

"Tell me about other times you've done this," he said.

I started sharing more examples of colleagues I'd helped navigate office politics, friends I'd guided through career transitions, the consulting situation I'd worked my way out of using strategic thinking.

"Jeremy," he said, setting down his coffee cup and looking at me directly, "do you realize what you're describing?"

I wasn't sure where he was going with this.

"You help people gain clarity. That's your superpower. And from what you're telling me, you have a repeatable process for doing it."

He leaned back in his chair, smiling. "This is incredible. You're sitting on something that could help people on a much grander scale."

He was recognizing what would become The CLARITY Code™, a systematic methodology for transforming complexity into clarity that I had been applying unconsciously but consistently.

The Challenge

"Think about it," he continued. "How many people do you know who feel stuck right now? Stuck in their careers, stuck in relationships, stuck trying to start businesses, stuck dealing with life challenges?"

I thought about it. The answer was: almost everyone I knew was stuck somewhere.

"And how many of them have access to someone who can help them think through their situation systematically and see possibilities they can't see on their own?"

The answer was: very few.

"You have a gift that most people desperately need. But you're only sharing it with people in your immediate circle. What if you could reach more people?"

He started describing what he saw when he looked at my approach. I wasn't just solving individual problems; I was helping people change their thoughts about their problems. I wasn't just giving advice but teaching people a framework for navigating complex situations.

"You could build a brand around this," he said, his excitement building. "Help people take positive steps on how to transform their confusion into clarity, whether that's professional challenges, relationship issues, starting businesses, accomplishing goals, or dealing with various life challenges."

The Vision

He pulled out his phone and showed me examples of people who had built platforms around helping others solve problems. Coaches, speakers, and authors who had taken their natural talents and scaled them to reach thousands of people.

"Your approach feels unique," he said. "Most people either give generic motivational advice or very specific tactical solutions. What you do is different; you help people see their situations differently and develop their own strategic solutions."

He talked about creating customized roadmaps for people, offering workshops and coaching programs, and building a community around the concept of gaining clarity.

"You could call it something like 'The Clarity Method,'" he suggested. "People would immediately understand what that means and why they need it."

I sat there, coffee getting cold, as he painted a picture of something I'd never seriously considered. Taking this natural talent I'd always taken for granted and turning it into something that could actually help people at scale.

The Resistance

"I don't know," I said. "This feels like something I just do naturally for friends and colleagues. Can you really build a business around that?"

"Jeremy," he said, "some of the most successful coaches and consultants in the world built their careers around systematizing their natural talents. The fact that it comes naturally to you doesn't make it less valuable—it makes it more valuable, because you can do it authentically."

He challenged some of my assumptions about what was possible.

"You think this is just being a good friend, but you're actually providing people with a framework for strategic thinking that most people never learn. That's incredibly valuable."

"You think anyone can do this, but I've been watching you describe your process, and it's sophisticated. You're naturally integrating systems thinking, strategic planning, resource optimization, and behavioral change. That's not common."

"You think it's not 'real' business because it feels easy to you, but that's exactly why it could be a great business. You're not forcing yourself to do something you're bad at, you're scaling something you're naturally excellent at."

The Turning Point

"Here's what I want you to do," he said as we were wrapping up. "Don't make any decisions today. But think about this: What would happen if you formalized your approach into an actual method that you could teach to other people?"

He suggested I start by reverse-engineering what I was already doing. "Take a few examples of times you've helped people gain clarity, and break down exactly what you did step by step. Look for the patterns. See if there's a systematic approach you can document and replicate."

"If you can do that," he said, "you'll know whether this is something that can be scaled. And if it can be scaled, you'll have a decision to make about what to do with that knowledge."

As we stood up to leave, he said something that would stick with me for months: "Jeremy, you have a talent that can genuinely change people's lives. The question isn't whether you should do something with it. The question is whether you can afford not to."

The Internal Shift

Walking back to my car, I felt something I hadn't experienced in a long time: excitement about a possibility I'd never seriously considered.

For years, I'd been focused on building my career, climbing the corporate ladder, following the traditional path to professional success. But what if there was a different path? What if I could build something around this natural talent that felt both personally fulfilling and professionally viable?

The more I thought about it, the more I realized he was right: I had a systematic approach. It wasn't random or intuitive; there were consistent steps I followed, consistent questions I asked, consistent ways I helped people reframe their situations.

I'd never thought about documenting that process because it felt so natural. But what if I could break it down into teachable components? What if I could create a framework that others could learn and apply to their stuck points?

That evening, I started doing exactly what my colleague had suggested. I opened a new document and began writing down specific examples of times I'd helped people gain clarity, breaking down each situation step by step.

The Documentation Process

I decided to use the STAR method* (Situation, Task, Action, Result) to analyze each example systematically. It was a framework I learned from the INROADS® program during my intern days, perfect for breaking down complex scenarios into understandable components for storytelling. It actually helped me get my first internship with The Coca-Cola Company.

* Dr. William C. Byham developed the STAR method.

For Marcus's government contract situation:

- **Situation**: He was stuck on pricing a government contract and felt overwhelmed by the complexity

- **Task**: Help him develop a confident pricing strategy based on real market data

- **Action**: Guided him through systematic research and value proposition development

- **Result**: He won the contract at his target price point and established himself as a credible expert

For David's career transition:

- **Situation**: He felt trapped between policy training and marketing passion, unsure how to make the transition

- **Task**: Help him see a clear path from his current reality to his desired career

- **Action**: Helped him recognize his natural talents, research transition options, and develop an implementation plan

- **Result**: He successfully transitioned to marketing strategy and is thriving in roles that align with his strengths

As I documented more examples, the pattern became undeniable. I followed a consistent sequence of steps, a systematic approach to helping people move from confusion to clarity.

I was beginning to see what my colleague had seen: this wasn't just natural helpfulness. This was a methodology.

If it were a methodology, it could be formalized, documented, and shared with people who needed it.

The question was: what would I call it, and how would I structure it so that others could learn and apply it?

That's when I remembered something from my spreadsheet exercise months earlier. When I'd been documenting my natural talents, one phrase had kept coming up: helping people gain "clarity."

What if I worked backward from that word? What if I created a framework that literally spelled out C-L-A-R-I-T-Y?

Sitting at my kitchen table that night, I started playing with possibilities. What would each letter represent? What were the essential steps in helping someone move from confusion to clarity?

I didn't have all the answers yet, but I had the beginning of something that felt important.

For the first time, I was thinking about my natural talent not just as something I did for friends, but as something that could potentially help many more people than I could reach through casual conversations and coffee chats.

The methodology was about to be born.

CHAPTER 7
THE METHOD EMERGES

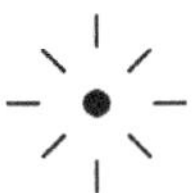

"Your unconscious competence becomes conscious power when you reverse-engineer your wins." ©

The breakthrough came at 2:47 AM on a Saturday night.

I know the exact time because I was sitting at my kitchen table, surrounded by pages of notes from my STAR analyses, when everything suddenly clicked into place. I'd been working for weeks to reverse-engineer my natural process, documenting example after example, looking for the underlying pattern that connected them all.

My coffee had gone cold hours ago. My wife was asleep upstairs. The house was completely quiet except for the occasional rustle of papers as I moved between different case studies, searching for the thread that would tie everything together.

And then, in one of those moments of clarity that only come when you've been wrestling with a problem long enough, I saw it.

The Recognition

It started with a simple observation: every time I'd successfully helped someone gain clarity, I'd unconsciously guided them through the same sequence of realizations.

With Marcus and his government contract, I'd started by helping him see his situation clearly—not just the pricing challenge, but the strategic communication problem he was actually solving. Then we'd gotten specific about what success would look like. We'd identified the real obstacles. We'd shifted his thinking about his value. We'd leveraged his existing assets. We'd created a systematic plan. And we'd built in ways to maintain momentum.

With David and his career transition, the pattern was identical. Current reality, clear destination, real obstacles, belief transformation, hidden resources, strategic action, sustainable momentum.

Looking back at my own consulting experience, I realized I'd unconsciously followed the same process. The difference was that I'd had to figure it out through months of trial and error rather than having someone guide me through it systematically.

Every successful intervention contained the same seven elements, though not always in perfect linear order. Sometimes we'd cycle back to earlier steps as new insights emerged, but all seven components were present in every breakthrough.

This was the birth of what would become The **CLARITY Code™**.

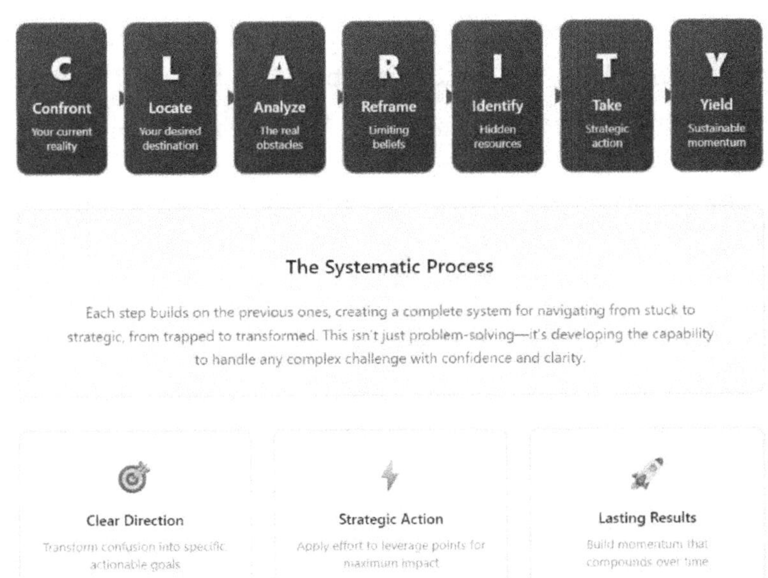

The Word Game

The word "CLARITY" had been bouncing around in my head since my conversation with my colleague weeks earlier. What if each letter could represent one of those essential steps?

I grabbed a fresh piece of paper and started playing with possibilities.

C could be about confronting your current situation or challenging your reality.

L could be about locating your goal or your destination.

A could be about assessing obstacles or analyzing them.

R could be about reframing differently or reframing beliefs.

I was clearly about identifying resources or illuminating what you already had available.

T could be about taking action or creating plans.

Y could be about yielding momentum or sustaining it.

I wrote and rewrote, trying different words, testing them against my documented examples. Some combinations felt forced. Others felt too generic. But gradually, something started to emerge that felt both natural and comprehensive.

C.L.A.R.I.T.Y.

- **Confront** your current reality
- **Locate** your desired destination
- **Analyze** the real obstacles
- **Reframe** limiting beliefs
- **Identify** hidden resources
- **Take** strategic action
- **Yield** sustainable momentum

I stared at the paper, feeling something I can only describe as recognition. This wasn't just a clever acronym, this was exactly what I'd been doing intuitively for years.

The Validation Process

Over the following hours, I tested the framework against every example I'd documented. Did Marcus's situation include all seven elements? Check. David's career transition? Check. My own consulting recovery? Check.

I started looking for counterexamples where I'd tried to help someone but hadn't succeeded. In every case, I could identify which steps had been skipped or rushed through.

There was the colleague who wanted to change careers but never got honest about why his current role wasn't working. We'd jumped straight to exploring options without confronting his real motivations. The advice felt hollow because it wasn't grounded in truth.

There was a friend who had a clear vision of starting her own business, but couldn't identify what was holding her back. We'd created elaborate action plans that she never implemented because we hadn't addressed her underlying fear of financial instability.

There was my own early attempt to solve the consulting situation by working harder rather than working smarter. I'd tried to create different outcomes without first reframing my beliefs about how corporate systems actually operated.

The framework wasn't just descriptive, it was predictive. It helped explain why some approaches worked while others didn't.

The Emotional Impact

Sitting there at nearly 3 AM, looking at my seven-step framework, I felt something profound shifting inside me.

For the first time, I had language for something I'd always done naturally. I had a structure for an approach that had felt intuitive but undefined. Most importantly, I had something that could potentially be taught to other people rather than requiring them to rely on my personal guidance.

This wasn't just about helping friends and colleagues anymore. This was about addressing one of the most universal human challenges, the experience of feeling stuck, trapped, or unable to move forward, in a systematic way that others could learn and apply.

I thought about my colleague's words: "You could help people on a grander scale."

For the first time, that possibility felt real.

I discovered The CLARITY Code™: a systematic methodology for transforming complexity into clarity, confusion into direction, and obstacles into opportunities.

Understanding the map is one thing; transforming complexity into clarity in your life is another.

The CLARITY Code™ offers you a systematic methodology, a proven framework for navigating any situation where you feel stuck or overwhelmed. But the journey from intellectual understanding to actual transformation requires more than just insight; it demands deliberate practice, structured application, and expert guidance for those inevitable moments when resistance emerges or the path seems unclear.

That's why, alongside this book, I've developed **The CLARITY Code™ Workbook**, your hands-on transformation companion filled with specific exercises, reflection prompts, and assessment tools designed to translate these seven principles into concrete progress in your actual situation. Every concept you're learning becomes an actionable step you can take immediately.

And for those moments when the process feels challenging or when you need deeper insights into your specific circumstances, **The CLARITY Navigator™** serves as your personal coaching companion, offering the kind of guidance and breakthrough perspectives I've provided to numerous colleagues and clients, anticipating your questions and helping you work through resistance with the same depth and precision you'd experience in our one-on-one sessions.

Think of them as your personal clarity toolkit, ensuring you're not just reading about transforming complexity into clarity but systematically experiencing it. Because understanding the method is just the beginning. Living it is where the real transformation happens.

The Questions That Emerged

But with that excitement came new questions that kept me awake even longer.

Could this framework really work when applied consciously rather than intuitively? I'd always relied on natural instincts to guide people through these conversations. Would it feel mechanical or artificial if I followed the steps deliberately?

Was the framework complete, or were there crucial elements I was missing? Seven steps felt comprehensive, but what if there were important nuances that couldn't be captured in a simple acronym?

Could other people learn to apply this approach effectively, or was it too dependent on natural coaching abilities and life experience?

Most importantly, was I ready to test this framework in a real situation where the stakes mattered?

The Anticipation

I had no idea the universe would provide the perfect test case.

My wife had been dealing with some frustration at work, but I hadn't paid much attention to the details. It seemed like typical workplace politics and bureaucratic challenges that most people face in their careers.

I didn't know yet that her situation was about to become far more complex—involving student loan forgiveness programs, political timing, organizational transitions, and personal fulfillment, all interconnected in ways that would require every element of strategic thinking I'd developed.

I didn't know that I was about to have the opportunity to apply my newly formalized framework to the most important person in my life, in a situation with real consequences that could affect our financial future and her career satisfaction.

And I definitely didn't know that this test case would prove not only that The CLARITY Code™ worked, but that it worked even when applied unconsciously by someone who truly understood its principles.

But that night, sitting in my kitchen with pages of notes scattered around me and a fresh framework written on a single sheet of paper, I felt something I hadn't experienced in a long time: complete clarity about a path forward.

I had identified something I was naturally good at, documented a systematic approach for doing it, and created a framework that could potentially help many more people than I could reach through individual conversations.

The methodology was born. Now I needed to understand how each piece actually worked.

It was time to dive deep into the mechanics of transforming complexity into clarity.

CHAPTER 8

C - CONFRONT: THE FOUNDATION OF ALL CHANGE

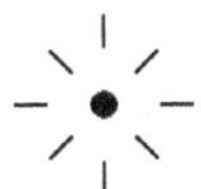

"The truth might punch you in the face, and for a second, even you won't buy your excuses." ©

Before any transformation can begin, you need to know your exact coordinates in the landscape of your life. And when you're feeling stuck, those coordinates are often obscured by denial, wishful thinking, and well-meaning self-deception. The most courageous step on the path to clarity isn't about moving forward, it's about having the audacity to see exactly where you stand right now. This is the power of 'C' in our method: the willingness to Confront your current reality with unflinching honesty.

Most people think they already know where they are. They can tell you about their job, relationships, financial situation, and goals. They can recite the facts of their circumstances with remarkable precision.

But there's a difference between knowing the facts of your situation and truly seeing your reality clearly.

The difference is what separates people who stay stuck from people who break through to something better.

My Story: The Brutal Truth About Corporate Prison

When I first started at that consulting firm, I thought I knew exactly where I was: a successful professional with an advanced degree, joining a prestigious company, ready to make my mark in healthcare consulting.

I had all the facts right. Big Four firm, check. Healthcare focus, check. The project manager who had recruited me, check. Opportunity for growth and travel, check.

But I was completely blind to my actual reality.

It took me three months of escalating frustration and systematic sabotage before I could admit what was happening. I wasn't just dealing with a difficult colleague or a challenging project. I was trapped in a system designed to keep me exactly where I was, working for someone whose career advancement depended on my failure.

The turning point came during one of my sleepless nights, about two months into the nightmare. I was lying in bed, replaying the day's interactions, when I finally asked myself a question I'd been avoiding:

"What if this isn't about my performance at all? What if this is about something completely different?"

That question opened the floodgates to a series of realizations I'd been unconsciously resisting:

- My colleague had zero healthcare experience, but was threatened by mine

- He was on the advisory side of the firm and needed to justify bringing in another advisory consultant instead of keeping me

- The client actually liked my suggestions, but deferred to his relationship and seniority

- My current coach had no influence within my business vertical and couldn't help me even if he wanted to

- The firm's culture prioritized internal politics over merit-based advancement

- I was playing a game whose rules nobody had explained to me

These weren't comfortable truths. Admitting them meant acknowledging that my usual approach of working harder and being more competent wasn't going to solve this problem. It meant accepting that I'd been naive about how corporate systems really work.

But it also meant I could finally stop spinning my wheels and start developing a strategy based on reality rather than wishful thinking.

This is the power of confronting your current reality: it transforms confusion into clarity by forcing you to see what is, rather than what you hope is or think should be.

The Principle: Why Truth Is the Foundation of All Change

Here's what I've learned about why the "Confront" step is so crucial: You cannot navigate from where you think you are, where you wish you were, or where you think you should be. You can only navigate from where you actually are.

This sounds obvious, but it's one of the hardest things for most people to do consistently. We have powerful psychological mechanisms that protect us from uncomfortable truths:

Minimization: "It's not really that bad. I'm probably just being too sensitive."

Rationalization: "There are good reasons why this situation exists. I just need to be more patient/understanding/flexible."

Comparison: "Other people have it worse than I do. I shouldn't complain."

Wishful Thinking: "Things will probably get better on their own if I just wait it out."

Identity Protection: "Admitting this situation is problematic would mean admitting I made poor choices, and I'm not someone who makes poor choices."

All of these mental habits serve important psychological functions, but they also keep us stuck in situations that aren't serving us.

The courage to see clearly isn't about being negative or pessimistic. It's about developing the emotional strength to look at your situation without the filters that make you feel better but prevent you from taking effective action.

In The CLARITY Code™, confronting reality isn't about judgment, it's about gathering accurate intelligence that enables strategic response.

The Process: How to Develop the Courage for Clear Seeing

Based on my experience helping dozens of people through this step, here's how to approach it systematically:

1. Create Emotional Safety

Before you can be honest about your situation, you need to create conditions where the truth won't overwhelm you.

This might mean:

- Choosing a time when you're calm and centered, not in the middle of a crisis

- Finding a private space where you won't be interrupted or judged

- Reminding yourself that seeing clearly is the first step toward improvement, not an endpoint

- Having support available (a trusted friend, therapist, or coach) for processing difficult realizations

2. Use the External Observer Technique

One of the most effective ways to cut through self-deception is to describe your situation as if you were observing someone else's life.

If your best friend were in your exact situation, how would you describe what was happening to them? What patterns would you notice? What advice would you give them?

This technique bypasses the ego protection mechanisms that distort our perception of our own circumstances.

3. Separate Facts from Stories

Facts are objective, verifiable observations. Stories are the interpretations, meanings, and explanations we attach to those facts.

For example:

- **Fact**: My coworker dismissed my suggestions in the meeting

- **Story**: He dismissed my suggestions because he doesn't respect my expertise

- **Alternative Story**: He dismissed my suggestions because my success threatens his promotion prospects

Getting clear about the facts helps you see what's actually happening versus what you're making it mean.

4. Look for Patterns, Not Just Events

Individual incidents can be explained away or dismissed as anomalies. However, patterns reveal underlying dynamics that need to be addressed.

In my consulting situation, I could have explained away any single incident of sabotage. But when I mapped out the pattern—email traps, blocked travel opportunities, systematic undermining, exclusion from information—the systemic nature of the problem became undeniable.

5. Examine Your Emotional Reactions

Strong emotional reactions often point to important truths we're trying to avoid.

If you find yourself getting defensive about certain aspects of your situation or notice you avoid thinking about specific areas of your life, those are usually signals that deeper examination is needed.

6. Do A Reality Check with Trusted Others

Sometimes we need external perspectives to see what we've become blind to.

Choose people who:

- Know you well enough to observe patterns in your life
- Care about you enough to tell you difficult truths
- Are you emotionally detached enough from your situation to be objective
- Have the wisdom and experience to provide a useful perspective

Ask them direct questions: What do you see that I might be missing? What patterns do you notice in how I talk about this situation? If you were in my position, what would concern you most?

7. Use Structured Assessment Tools

Sometimes, a formal assessment can reveal truths that casual reflection misses.

This might include:

- Rating your satisfaction in different life areas on a 1-10 scale
- Tracking your emotions and energy levels for a week
- Completing a values assessment to see where your life is or isn't aligned

- Writing a "day in the life" description of your current reality
- Creating a timeline of how your situation has evolved over time

Common Resistance Points and How to Navigate Them

"I Already Know My Situation"

If this step feels unnecessary because you think you already see your situation clearly, that's often a sign you most need it. The people who are most resistant to honest assessment are usually the ones with the most blind spots.

Try this: Write a detailed description of your situation, then put it away for a week. Come back and read it as if someone else wrote it. What do you notice?

"I Don't Want to Be Negative"

Honest assessment isn't about being negative, it's about being accurate. You can acknowledge problems without becoming pessimistic about solutions.

Reframe this step as "gathering intelligence" rather than "focusing on problems." You're not dwelling on what's wrong; you're collecting the information you need to make good decisions.

"What If the Truth Is Too Overwhelming?"

Sometimes people avoid honest assessment because they fear what they might discover. But here's the thing: the truth of your situation exists whether you acknowledge it or not. Avoiding it doesn't make it less real, it just makes you less equipped to deal with it.

Start small. Pick one area of your life that feels manageable to examine honestly. Build your tolerance for truth-telling gradually.

"I Don't Know How to Change It, So Why Look?"

This is putting the cart before the horse. You don't need to know how to solve a problem before you're willing to acknowledge it exists. In fact, trying to solve problems you haven't clearly defined usually leads to wasted effort and increased frustration.

The goal of this step isn't to solve anything; it's simply to see clearly. Solutions come later in the process.

Why This Step Is Non-Negotiable

Every other step in The CLARITY Code™ depends on the foundation of clear seeing. If you're not honest about your current reality:

- You can't create an accurate vision of where you want to go (Step L)

- You can't identify the real obstacles preventing progress (Step A)

- You can't transform the beliefs that are actually limiting you (Step R)

- You can't leverage the resources you actually have available (Step I)

- You can't create action plans that address your real situation (Step T)

- You can't build momentum that will actually be sustainable (Step Y)

This is why gaining clarity always begins with the courage to see clearly, even when, especially when, the truth is uncomfortable.

In my consulting situation, everything changed once I stopped trying to make the situation work and started seeing it for what it was: a political problem requiring a political solution.

That honesty didn't solve the problem immediately, but it gave me something I hadn't had before: an accurate map of the territory I needed to navigate.

And you can't find your way out of anywhere until you first know where you really are.

CHAPTER 9

L - LOCATE: THE POWER OF PRECISE VISION

"Your dreams don't need more passion, they need more pixels." ©

Imagine setting your GPS to "somewhere better." That's how most people approach their dreams, with vague hopes for improvement but no specific coordinates for success. As my friend David's remarkable transformation reveals, the difference between wandering and arriving lies in one critical shift: moving from abstract wishes to laser-focused vision.

This chapter unveils the transformative power of "L" in The CLARITY Code™: how to Locate your desired destination with the precision that turns dreams into inevitabilities.

The Breakthrough Moment

You'll recall that David felt trapped between his policy training and his natural passion for event planning and relationship building. His initial goal was frustratingly vague: "I want something more fulfilling." This is like telling your GPS to take you "somewhere nice"; it can't give you directions because it doesn't know the destination.

The breakthrough didn't happen by just acknowledging his unhappiness. It happened when we moved from the vague to the vivid.

"Let's say you could design your ideal career," I said during that networking event. "Not just 'something fulfilling,' but exactly what you'd be doing day to day. What would that look like?"

David's answer became the seed of his transformation: "I'd want to be developing marketing strategies for organizations I believe in. Creating campaigns that connect people with experiences that genuinely improve their lives. Working with teams that value creativity and innovation, where I could use my event planning skills and relationship-building abilities as core business functions."

That specificity changed everything. Instead of wandering around hoping something better would appear, David now had coordinates for his GPS. He could research MBA programs focused on marketing strategy, network with people in that field, and create a systematic plan for transitioning from policy work to his ideal role.

Today, David does exactly what he envisioned during that conversation. He develops marketing strategies for organizations he believes in, creates campaigns that connect people with meaningful experiences, and uses his natural talents as core business functions.

The difference between his stuck state and his current success wasn't just hard work or good luck; it was the precision of his destination.

The Principle: Why Vague Goals Create Vague Results

David's transformation illustrates a fundamental truth about how vision works: the specificity of your destination directly determines the power of your pull toward it.

Here's why precise vision is so crucial:

1. Clarity Enables Decision-Making

When you have only a vague sense of wanting "something better," every opportunity looks roughly the same. You can't distinguish between options because you don't have clear criteria for evaluation.

Once you get specific about your destination, you can quickly assess whether any given opportunity moves you toward or away from your target.

2. Precision Activates Problem-Solving

Vague goals generate vague strategies. "Find a more fulfilling career" doesn't suggest any particular approach or next steps.

"Get into a top MBA program to transition into marketing strategy roles" immediately suggests specific actions: research programs, study for standardized tests, network with alumni, and craft compelling applications.

3. Specific Vision Engages Others

When you talk about wanting "something better," people don't know how to help you. The goal is too abstract to generate useful advice or connections.

When you can articulate a specific vision, people immediately think of relevant contacts, helpful resources, and specific opportunities.

4. Measurable Targets Create Momentum

You can't track progress toward vague aspirations. Without measurable progress, motivation naturally decreases over time.

Specific destinations provide concrete milestones that create evidence of progress and fuel for continued effort.

5. Detailed Vision Activates the Subconscious

When you can see, feel, and experience your desired future in vivid detail, your subconscious mind works toward it even when you're not consciously focused.

You begin noticing relevant opportunities, positioning yourself strategically, and making choices that support your vision, not through forced effort, but through the natural result of clear intention.

In The CLARITY Code™, locating your destination isn't about wishful thinking; it's about creating a target so clear that your mind can't help but move toward it.

The Process: How to Create Compelling, Specific Visions

Based on my experience helping people move from vague aspirations to precise destinations, here's how to approach this step systematically:

1. Start with Feeling, Then Add Specifics

Most people try to logic their way into vision, but that often produces goals that sound reasonable but don't generate emotional pull.

Instead, start by identifying how you want to feel in your ideal situation. Energized? Challenged? Creative? Peaceful? Connected? Autonomous?

Once you're clear on the emotional quality of your desired experience, you can work backward to identify specific circumstances that would generate those feelings.

2. Use the "Day in the Life" Technique

Write a detailed description of a typical day in your ideal future, told in the present tense as if you're already living it.

Include:

- What time you wake up, and how you feel
- What your physical environment looks like
- Who you interact with and how those interactions feel
- What specific activities fill your time
- What challenges you're facing and how you approach them
- How you feel at the end of the day

This exercise often reveals preferences and priorities that abstract goal-setting misses.

3. Apply the "5 Whys" Technique

For any goal you're considering, ask "Why do I want this?" Then ask why you want whatever you just identified. Continue this process for five levels.

This technique helps distinguish between goals you think you should want and goals that connect to your deeper motivations.

4. Test Vision Specificity

A well-formed vision should be specific enough that you could:

- Explain it clearly to someone else in two minutes
- Identify concrete evidence that would prove you'd achieved it
- Distinguish opportunities that move you toward it from those that don't
- Create a reasonable timeline for achieving it
- Identify specific obstacles that might prevent it

If your vision doesn't meet these criteria, it needs more development.

5. Include Multiple Dimensions

Comprehensive vision includes:

- **Professional aspects**: What type of work, with whom, in what context
- **Personal aspects**: Relationships, lifestyle, location, experiences
- **Financial aspects**: Income, security, freedom, impact
- **Growth aspects**: Learning, challenge, contribution, legacy
- **Values aspects**: How your vision honors what matters most to you

6. Make It Compelling But Believable

Your vision should be inspiring enough to motivate sustained effort but believable enough that your subconscious mind accepts it as possible.

If your vision feels too small, you won't be motivated to pursue it. If it feels too large, you'll unconsciously sabotage your efforts because part of you doesn't believe it's achievable.

Common Vision Pitfalls and How to Avoid Them

"I Don't Know What I Want"

This usually means you're trying to figure it out intellectually rather than connecting with what actually energizes you.

Try this: Instead of asking "What do I want?" ask "What activities make me lose track of time?" or "When do I feel most like myself?"

"My Vision Isn't Realistic"

Often, this is a limiting belief disguised as practical thinking. Before dismissing a vision as unrealistic, research whether other people have achieved similar outcomes.

If they have, your vision is realistic, you just need to understand the path.

"I Have Too Many Options"

When everything feels equally appealing, it usually means you haven't gotten specific enough about what matters most to you.

Try the "forced ranking" exercise: If you could only achieve one of your goals, which would you choose? Then, if you could achieve two, what would be second? Continue until you have clear priorities.

"My Vision Keeps Changing"

Some evolution is natural as you learn more about yourself and your options. But constant shifting often indicates a lack of connection to deeper values.

Focus on identifying the underlying values and experiences you want, then allow the specific expression of those values to evolve.

The Vision-Action Bridge

The power of precise vision isn't just psychological, it's practical. When David moved from "I want fulfillment" to "I want to develop marketing strategies using my event planning and relationship-building skills," everything else became possible.

He could research specific MBA programs. He could network with marketing professionals. He could craft application essays that positioned his unique background as an asset. He could measure progress through concrete milestones: GMAT scores, application deadlines, interview invitations, and acceptance letters.

Most importantly, he could maintain motivation through the inevitable challenges because he had a clear picture of where he was heading and why it mattered to him.

This is the transformative power of precisely locating your destination: it converts wandering into navigation, wishful thinking into strategic planning, and vague hopes into achievable outcomes.

Why This Step Is Crucial for Everything That Follows

Everything else in The CLARITY Code™ depends on having a clear destination:

- You can't identify the real obstacles (Step A) without knowing where you're trying to go

- You can't transform limiting beliefs (Step R) without a compelling alternative to move toward

- You can't recognize relevant resources (Step I) without clarity about what you're trying to achieve

- You can't create effective action plans (Step T) without specific targets to aim for

- You can't maintain momentum (Step Y) without measurable progress toward meaningful goals

In David's case, everything became possible once he moved from vague aspiration to precise vision. That clarity didn't just illuminate his path—it activated every other step in the process of gaining clarity.

And that's the power of locating your destination with specificity: it transforms wandering into navigation, confusion into direction, and dreams into achievable outcomes.

CHAPTER 10

A - ANALYZE: OBSTACLES AS INFORMATION

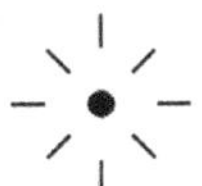

"Your obstacles aren't roadblocks, they're billboards advertising exactly what you're not ready to face." ©

What if the very forces blocking your path weren't just impediments, but intelligence? Most of us encounter obstacles and immediately shift into battle mode, strategizing how to overcome, outmaneuver, or simply power through. But hidden within every barrier lies critical data about what you need to learn, develop, or understand to move forward.

This chapter explores the profound insight of "A" in our framework: how to Analyze obstacles not as enemies to defeat, but as messengers carrying precisely the information you need for a breakthrough.

My Story: The Difference Between Obvious and Real

I was completely focused on the wrong obstacle for the first three months of my consulting nightmare.

The obvious obstacle was clear to everyone: I was dealing with a difficult coworker who was sabotaging my work. He dismissed my suggestions, blocked my access to information, excluded me from opportunities, and systematically undermined my reputation with clients and project leadership.

Every conversation I had about the situation focused on this obvious barrier. Friends offered advice about how to deal with difficult people. Mentors suggested strategies for building rapport with a challenging coworker. My colleague encouraged me to document his behavior and report it to management.

All of this advice was well-intentioned, but it was aimed at the wrong target.

The breakthrough came during one of my sleepless nights, about three months into the situation. I was lying in bed, replaying the day's frustrations, when I finally asked myself a different question:

"What if this guy's behavior isn't the real obstacle? What if he's just a symptom of something deeper?"

That question opened up an entirely different analysis of my situation.

The Systemic Discovery

Once I stopped focusing on his individual behavior and started looking at the larger system, the real obstacles became visible:

Obstacle 1: I didn't understand how power and influence actually operated within the firm. I'd been assuming that merit and client satisfaction would naturally lead to career advancement. However, the firm's culture prioritized internal relationships and political navigation over technical competence.

Obstacle 2: I lacked access to the informal networks that drove real decision-making. The organizational chart showed one power structure, but the actual influence patterns were completely different. My official coach had zero clout in my business vertical.

Obstacle 3: I was operating from a fundamentally incorrect mental model about how consulting firms work. I thought I was in a meritocracy where good work would be recognized and rewarded. In reality, I was in a complex social and political system where relationship management was as important as client delivery.

Obstacle 4: My presence on the team created a structural conflict that had nothing to do with my performance. He needed to justify hiring another advisory consultant, and my success would undermine that justification. This wasn't personal—it was systemic.

Obstacle 5: The firm's project assignment system was designed to keep consultants in place regardless of fit or performance. "When you're assigned to a project, you stay until they're finished with you" wasn't just a cultural norm—it was a structural feature that prevented people from escaping toxic situations.

This analysis revealed something crucial: the obvious obstacle (his difficult behavior) was actually the least important one. Even if he had suddenly become supportive and collaborative, I still would have been stuck because I didn't understand how to navigate the underlying system.

This discovery became a cornerstone of The CLARITY Code™: surface obstacles are often symptoms of deeper systemic issues requiring completely different approaches.

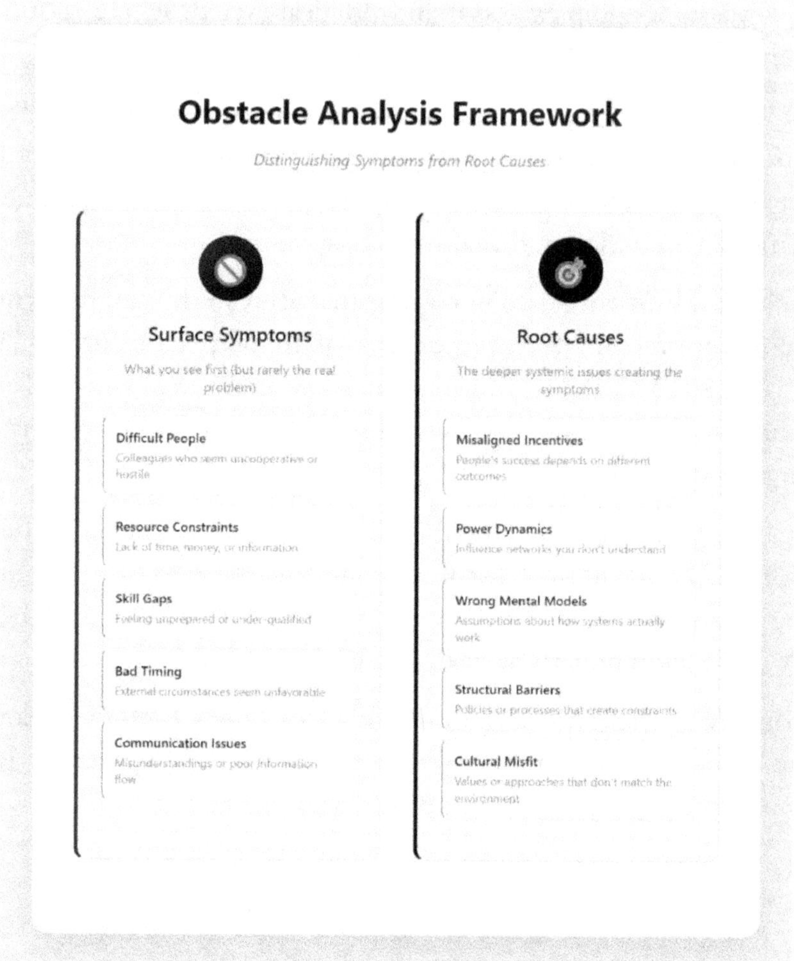

The Information Each Obstacle Provided

Once I started viewing obstacles as information sources rather than just barriers, each one revealed specific guidance about what I needed to develop:

From Obstacle 1, I learned I needed to study organizational dynamics and understand how influence really worked in corporate environments.

From Obstacle 2, I learned I needed to build strategic relationships with people who had actual decision-making power in my business vertical.

From Obstacle 3, I learned I needed to update my mental models about how complex organizations actually operate versus how they appear to operate.

From Obstacle 4, I learned I needed to recognize when my success threatened other people's interests and develop strategies for managing those conflicts.

From Obstacle 5, I learned I needed to understand the formal and informal rules that governed career mobility within the firm's culture.

Each obstacle wasn't just a problem to solve; it was a curriculum for development. The stuck situation taught me skills I would need to navigate complex organizational challenges throughout my career.

The Strategic Shift

This reframe completely changed my approach to the situation.

Instead of trying to change or overcome the obvious obstacle (his behavior), I focused on addressing the real obstacles (my lack of understanding about how the system actually worked).

I stopped trying to prove my competence through better work and started building strategic relationships with people who had influence.

I stopped expecting merit to speak for itself and started learning how to navigate organizational politics effectively.

I stopped viewing the situation as unfair and started treating it as an education about how complex systems operate.

Most importantly, I stopped trying to make the current situation work and started systematically creating conditions for a strategic exit.

This shift led directly to my coaching strategy, my successful transition to a different project, and ultimately to a much deeper understanding of how to navigate any complex organizational challenge.

The Principle: How Obstacles Reveal What You Need to Learn

My consulting experience illustrates a fundamental truth about obstacles: they're rarely what they appear to be on the surface.

The obvious obstacles, the difficult people, the resource constraints, the time pressures, and the skill gaps are usually symptoms of deeper systemic issues. When properly understood, those deeper issues reveal exactly what you need to develop to solve your current challenge and handle similar challenges more effectively in the future.

Here's how obstacles function as information:

1. They Reveal Blind Spots

The obstacles that surprise or frustrate you most often point to areas where your understanding of the situation is incomplete.

In my case, being blindsided by organizational politics revealed that I had huge blind spots about how corporate systems actually work versus how they're supposed to work.

2. They Identify Missing Capabilities

Obstacles often highlight skills, knowledge, or abilities you need to develop.

My inability to navigate the consulting firm's influence networks showed me I needed to develop political awareness and relationship-building capabilities I'd never prioritized before.

3. They Expose Limiting Mental Models

When your approach isn't working despite significant effort, obstacles often reveal that your mental model of the situation is inaccurate.

I'd been operating from a "meritocracy" model when the actual system ran on relationship and influence dynamics I didn't understand.

4. They Show You the Real Game Being Played

Sometimes obstacles reveal that you're playing by one set of rules while others are playing by completely different rules.

I was playing "deliver excellent client work" while others were playing "manage internal relationships and advance personal interests."

5. They Point to Necessary Growth

The obstacles that feel most overwhelming often indicate areas where you have the most potential for development.

Learning to navigate complex organizational dynamics became one of my most valuable professional capabilities, but I never would have developed it without the pressure of that stuck situation.

In The CLARITY Code™, analyzing obstacles isn't about overcoming barriers, it's about decoding the intelligence they contain about what you need to develop next.

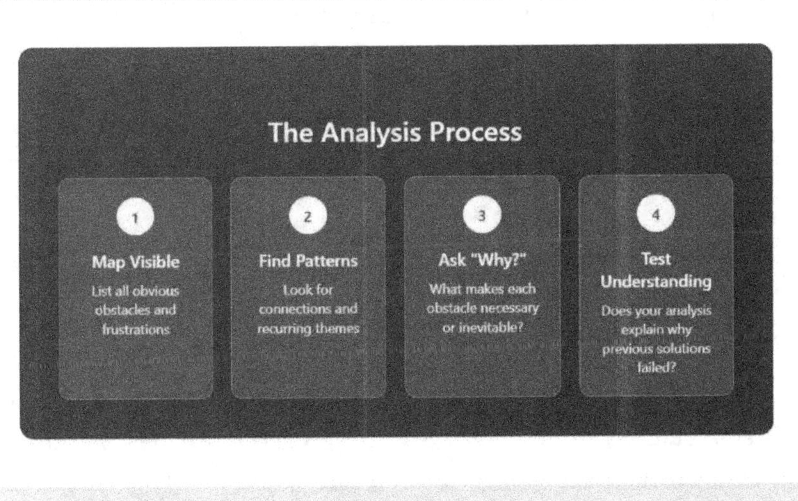

The Process: Distinguishing Symptoms from Root Causes

Based on my experience helping people analyze their obstacles systematically, here's how to distinguish between obvious barriers and real systemic issues:

1. Map All Visible Obstacles

Start by listing every obstacle you can identify, no matter how obvious or minor. Include:

- People who are difficult or unsupportive

- Resource constraints (time, money, information, tools)

- Skill or knowledge gaps

- Organizational or systemic barriers

- Environmental or circumstantial challenges

- Internal obstacles (fears, beliefs, habits, patterns)

2. Look for Interconnections

Draw lines between obstacles that seem related or that reinforce each other. Ask:

- Which obstacles create or maintain other obstacles?

- Are there "keystone obstacles" that, if addressed, would weaken several others?

- What patterns do you notice in how obstacles relate to each other?

3. Identify the Persistent Ones

Which obstacles keep showing up despite your efforts to address them? Persistent obstacles often point to deeper systemic issues rather than surface-level problems.

4. Ask "What Does This Require Me to Learn?"

For each major obstacle, ask:

- What capability would make this obstacle irrelevant?

- What understanding would change how I approach this challenge?

- What skill would turn this obstacle into an advantage?

- What perspective would make this obstacle less threatening?

5. Look for the Obstacle Behind the Obstacle

When you've identified what seems like the main barrier, ask:

- What makes this obstacle possible?

- What system or structure maintains this obstacle?

- If this obvious obstacle disappeared, what would be the next barrier?

- What would I need to be different about myself or my situation to make this obstacle irrelevant?

6. Test Your Analysis

A good obstacle analysis should:

- Explain why previous approaches haven't worked

- Suggest new strategies that address root causes rather than symptoms

- Identify specific capabilities or understanding you need to develop

- Reveal why this stuck point emerged at this particular time

- Point toward solutions that would prevent similar problems in the future

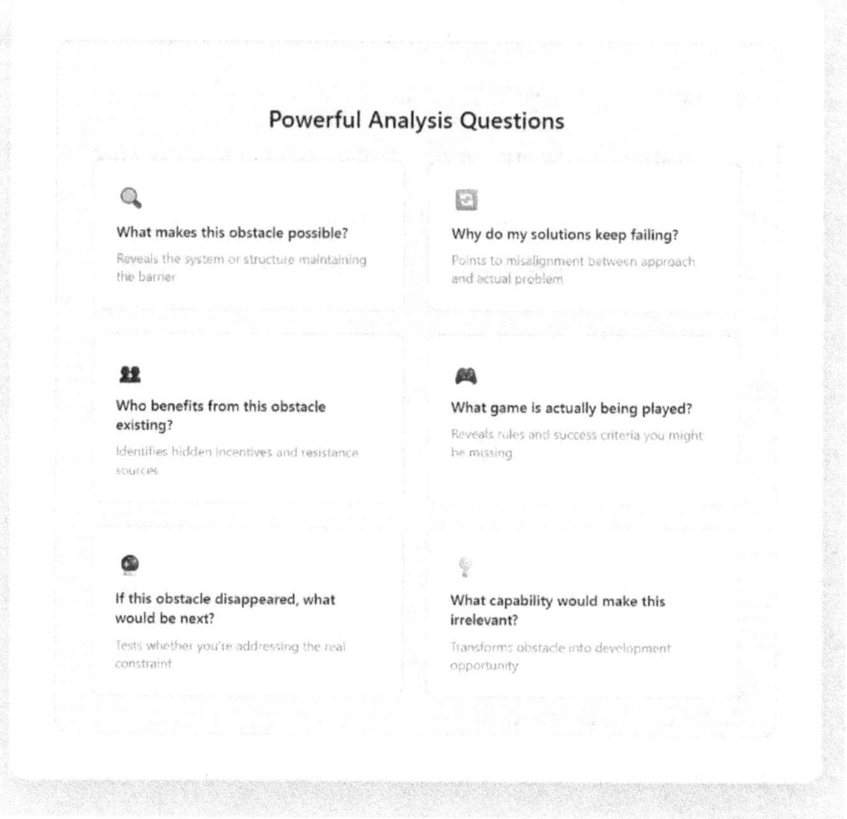

Common Obstacle Analysis Mistakes

Focusing Only on External Barriers

Many people identify obstacles only in their environment or circumstances while ignoring internal barriers like limiting beliefs, knowledge gaps, or skill deficits.

Effective analysis includes both external and internal obstacles, recognizing that changing your internal approach often transforms external barriers.

Personalizing Systemic Issues

When obstacles involve other people's behavior, it's easy to make it about personal conflicts rather than recognizing structural or systemic dynamics.

Ask: "If I were replaced by someone else in this situation, would they face the same obstacles?" If yes, the issue is systemic, not personal.

Stopping at the Surface Level

Most people identify obvious obstacles but don't dig deeper to understand the systems or dynamics that create those obstacles.

The question isn't just "What's in my way?" but "What makes this obstacle necessary or inevitable given the current system?"

Assuming All Obstacles Must Be Overcome

Sometimes the most effective approach isn't removing an obstacle but finding a way around it or even using it to your advantage.

Ask: "How might this obstacle actually serve my goals if I approached it differently?"

Why This Step Is Critical for Sustainable Solutions

Understanding obstacles as information sources rather than just barriers fundamentally changes how you approach gaining clarity:

1. It Reveals Why You're Stuck

Most people know they're stuck but don't understand why their previous efforts haven't worked. Proper obstacle analysis explains the mechanics of being stuck.

2. It Identifies the Real Work to Be Done

Instead of trying to work harder at ineffective approaches, you can focus on developing the specific capabilities the obstacles are pointing toward.

3. It Prevents Recurring Stuck Points

When addressing root causes rather than symptoms, you often solve entire categories of problems rather than individual incidents.

4. It Transforms Obstacles into Curriculum

Instead of viewing challenges as unfair or overwhelming, you can see them as precisely targeted development opportunities.

5. It Builds Systematic Problem-Solving Capabilities

Learning to analyze obstacles systematically gives you a framework for navigating any complex challenge you encounter in the future.

In my consulting situation, the obvious obstacle (difficult coworker) was actually the least important factor in my stuck scenario. The real obstacles were my lack of understanding of organizational dynamics, my missing relationships with influential people, and my incorrect mental models about how complex systems work.

Addressing those real obstacles not only solved my immediate problem but gave me capabilities I've used successfully in every complex situation since then.

That's why analyzing obstacles correctly is so crucial: it ensures that the work you do to gain clarity also prepares you to handle whatever challenges come next.

The obstacles aren't just in your way, they're showing you the way forward.

CHAPTER 11
R - REFRAME: CHANGING YOUR OPERATING SYSTEM

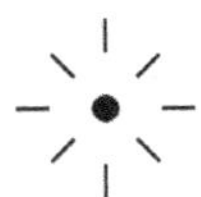

"Your limiting beliefs aren't protecting you, they're imprisoning you." ©

We often assume our greatest challenges are external, difficult circumstances, uncooperative people, or limited resources. But the most persistent barriers to clarity live within us: the deeply held beliefs that operate like invisible guardrails, quietly directing every choice we make. Like an outdated operating system running on powerful hardware, limiting beliefs constrain what we can accomplish regardless of our actual capabilities. In this chapter, we master the art of "R": how to Reframe those subconscious constraints and upgrade your internal programming for unlimited possibilities.

This is why willpower alone rarely creates lasting change. You can force yourself to take new actions, but if underlying beliefs remain unchanged, you'll eventually revert to behaviors that align with those beliefs. It's like trying to run new software on an outdated operating system; the system will either reject the new programs or cause them to malfunction.

The goal of this step isn't just to think more positively; it's to reconstruct the foundational beliefs upon which your entire approach to challenges is built.

My Story: From Victim of Politics to Student of Systems

The most profound transformation in my consulting experience wasn't learning new tactics for navigating organizational dynamics. It was a fundamental shift in how I understood my relationship to complex systems and challenging situations.

For the first few months, my internal narrative was entirely focused on victimhood:

"This guy is sabotaging me for no good reason."

"The system is unfair and designed to protect people like him."

"No matter how hard I work or how good my results are, politics will always win over merit."

"I'm trapped in a situation where success is impossible because the rules keep changing."

"People like me who believe in working hard and doing good work will always be taken advantage of by people who are willing to play political games."

These beliefs felt completely justified by my experience. After all, I was being sabotaged. The system did seem unfair. Merit wasn't being rewarded. The rules were unclear and seemed to change based on personal relationships rather than objective criteria.

But while these beliefs felt accurate, they were also incredibly disempowering. They positioned me as someone to whom things happened, rather than someone who could influence outcomes. They focused my attention on everything I couldn't control while blinding me to the things I could control.

Most importantly, they prevented me from seeing the situation as a learning opportunity rather than just a problem to survive.

This is the insidious nature of limiting beliefs: they feel true because they're based on real experience, but they constrain our ability to see possibilities beyond that experience.

The Shift Begins

The first crack in my victim narrative came during one of my conversations with a fellow consultant who had successfully navigated similar challenges.

"You know," he said, "every complex organization has formal rules and informal rules. The people who succeed learn both sets. The people who struggle only pay attention to one set or the other."

"What do you mean?" I asked.

"The formal rules are what they tell you in orientation and what's written in the employee handbook. The informal rules are how things actually work, who really makes decisions, what behavior gets rewarded, how to build influence, where the real power centers are."

"That sounds like politics," I said, with all the disdain I could muster.

"Maybe," he said. "Or maybe it's just understanding how human systems actually operate versus how we wish they operated."

That conversation planted a seed that would fundamentally change how I viewed not just my current situation, but every complex challenge I would face for the rest of my career.

The Belief Transformation

Over the following weeks, I began to consciously examine and challenge the beliefs that were keeping me stuck:

Old Belief: "I'm a victim of unfair politics." **New Belief**: "I'm a student learning how complex systems actually work."

This shift changed everything about how I approached the situation. Instead of feeling powerless and resentful, I became curious and strategic.

Instead of focusing on what was being done to me, I focused on what I could learn about how organizational dynamics really functioned.

Old Belief: "Merit should speak for itself." **New Belief**: "Merit needs to be combined with strategic thinking to create results."

This reframe helped me understand that my technical competence was necessary but not sufficient for success in complex environments. I needed to develop relationship-building and influence skills that I'd previously dismissed as unnecessary or beneath me.

Old Belief: "People who succeed through relationships rather than pure competence are somehow cheating." **New Belief**: "Understanding how to build productive relationships is itself a form of competence."

This shift allowed me to see networking and political awareness as legitimate skills to develop rather than distasteful necessities to endure.

Old Belief: "If I just keep my head down and do good work, eventually people will recognize my value." **New Belief**: "Creating value and ensuring that value is recognized are two different but equally important capabilities."

This belief change helped me understand that visibility and relationship-building weren't distractions from my real work—they were essential components of my real work.

Old Belief: "This situation is unfair and shouldn't be happening to me." **New Belief**: "This situation is teaching me skills I'll need for navigating complex challenges throughout my career."

This was perhaps the most powerful shift. It transformed the entire experience from something that was happening to me into something that was happening for me. Instead of a crisis to survive, it became a curriculum to complete.

In The CLARITY Code™, reframing beliefs isn't about positive thinking; it's about adopting more empowering and accurate interpretations of reality that enable strategic response.

The Practical Impact

These belief changes weren't just psychological comfort; they led to completely different actions and strategies:

The victim's beliefs had led me to focus on documenting the unfairness, complaining to anyone who would listen, and hoping that someone in authority would intervene to make the situation fairer.

The student's beliefs led me to study the firm's power dynamics, build strategic relationships with influential people, and develop a systematic plan for improving my situation through my own actions.

The victim's beliefs made every day feel like an endurance test where success meant surviving until something external changed.

The student's beliefs made every interaction a learning opportunity where success meant gathering intelligence and building capabilities that would serve me long after this particular challenge was resolved.

The Compound Effect

The most profound impact of this belief transformation became clear months later, after I'd successfully transitioned to a new project and was thriving in my role.

I realized that the beliefs I'd developed weren't just helpful for that one situation; they had fundamentally changed how I approached any complex challenge:

Instead of asking "Why is this happening to me?" I now asked, "What is this teaching me?"

Instead of looking for someone to blame, I looked for systems to understand.

Instead of hoping external circumstances would change, I focused on what I could learn or develop to handle the situation more effectively.

Instead of viewing obstacles as evidence that success was impossible, I viewed them as information about what capabilities I needed to develop.

This shift in mental operating system didn't just solve my consulting problem—it gave me a framework for navigating any situation where I felt stuck, overwhelmed, or powerless.

The Principle: How Beliefs Shape What You Can See and Do

My experience illustrates a fundamental truth about belief transformation: your beliefs don't just affect how you feel about your situation; they literally determine what options you can see and what actions seem possible.

Here's how limiting beliefs create and maintain stuck points:

1. They Filter Perception

Beliefs act like search algorithms, determining what information you notice and what you ignore. When I believed I was a victim of unfair politics, I noticed every instance of unfairness while missing opportunities to build relationships or demonstrate value strategically.

2. They Constrain Imagination

Beliefs about what's possible limit the range of solutions you can even conceive. My belief that "merit should speak for itself" prevented me from imagining strategies that combined competence with relationship building.

3. They Shape Behavior

You naturally act in ways that are consistent with your beliefs, even when those actions are counterproductive. My victim beliefs led to complaining and documenting unfairness, which actually weakened my position rather than improving it.

4. They Create Self-Fulfilling Prophecies

Beliefs influence your actions, creating results that confirm the original beliefs. My belief that "the system is rigged against people like me" led to behaviors that made me less successful.

5. They Determine Meaning

The same facts can support completely different beliefs depending on what meaning you assign to them. His sabotage could mean "I'm powerless" or "I need to understand the game being played." Both interpretations were factually accurate but led to entirely different outcomes.

The Process: Systematic Belief Transformation

Based on my experience helping people identify and transform the beliefs that keep them stuck, here's how to approach this step systematically:

1. Identify Your Limiting Beliefs

Most limiting beliefs operate below conscious awareness. To bring them into the light:

Complete these statements:

- "I can't [achieve my goal] because..."
- "Someone like me doesn't..."
- "I've always struggled with..."
- "To succeed, I would need to be more..."
- "I'm afraid that if I try, I'll..."

Listen to your internal dialogue during challenging moments. What do you tell yourself about why things aren't working?

Notice your emotional reactions. Strong negative emotions often signal beliefs that are being challenged or confirmed.

2. Trace Belief Origins

Understanding where limiting beliefs came from helps reduce their emotional grip:

- When did you first begin believing this?
- Who or what influenced you to adopt this belief?
- What experiences seemed to confirm this belief?
- How might this belief have protected you in the past?
- What function does this belief serve now?

3. Examine the Evidence

Most limiting beliefs contain some truth, but overgeneralize from limited experience:

- What evidence supports this belief?
- What evidence contradicts this belief?
- Are there exceptions to this belief that you've been ignoring?
- How might someone who disagrees with this belief interpret the same evidence?
- What assumptions are embedded in this belief that you're treating as facts?

4. Find Empowering Alternatives

Effective belief transformation doesn't ignore reality; it finds more empowering ways to interpret reality:

- What's a more empowering way to view this situation?
- How might someone who has succeeded in similar circumstances think about this challenge?
- What belief would be more helpful while still being believable?

- What would you need to believe to take the actions that success requires?

5. Test the New Belief

Beliefs become real through action, not just thinking:

- What would you do differently if you fully believed the empowering alternative?

- What small experiment could you try to test whether the new belief leads to better outcomes?

- How can you act "as if" the new belief is true, even if you're not completely convinced yet?

6. Reinforce Through Experience

New beliefs become established through repeated confirmation:

- Look for evidence that supports your new belief

- Notice that acting from the new belief creates better outcomes

- Surround yourself with people who naturally embody the empowering belief

- Create reminders that help you remember the new perspective during challenging moments

Common Belief Transformation Challenges

"But My Belief Is True"

Often, limiting beliefs contain some factual accuracy, which makes them harder to transform. The goal isn't to ignore reality but to find more empowering ways to interpret reality.

Instead of changing facts, change the meaning you assign to those facts. Instead of "I failed because I'm not good enough," try "I failed because I hadn't yet developed the skills this challenge required."

"I Don't Want to Be Unrealistic"

Some people resist belief transformation because they think it means becoming naive or overly optimistic. But empowering beliefs can be both realistic and useful.

The question isn't whether a belief is true in some absolute sense, but whether it's helpful for creating the outcomes you want.

"This Feels Like Self-Deception"

Changing beliefs can feel artificial at first, especially if you've held limiting beliefs for a long time. This discomfort is normal and temporary.

Remember that your current beliefs were also learned through experience and repetition. New beliefs will feel more natural as you gain experience acting from them.

"What If I Become Arrogant or Complacent?"

Some people worry that empowering beliefs will make them overconfident or lazy. However, truly empowering beliefs usually increase both confidence and motivation to grow.

The goal isn't to believe you're perfect, but to believe you're capable of learning and developing whatever you need to handle your challenges effectively.

Why This Step Is Essential for Lasting Change

Belief transformation is the foundation that makes all other changes sustainable:

- **Without addressing limiting beliefs**, you might temporarily change your actions, but you'll eventually revert to patterns that align with your underlying worldview.

- **Without empowering beliefs**, you might identify opportunities but won't have the confidence to pursue them effectively.

- **Without transformed thinking**, you might develop new skills, but you won't apply them in situations where they're most needed.

- **Without updated mental models**, you might create action plans, but they won't persist when those plans encounter inevitable obstacles.

In my consulting situation, the tactical changes—networking strategically, building relationships with influential people, and understanding organizational dynamics- were all important. But they only became possible after I transformed the beliefs that had been keeping me trapped in victim thinking.

The shift from "I'm being treated unfairly" to "I'm learning how complex systems work" didn't just solve my immediate problem. It gave me a mental operating system that has helped me navigate every complex challenge since then.

That's the power of belief transformation: it doesn't just change how you handle your current stuck point; it upgrades how you approach any difficult situation for the rest of your life.

Your beliefs are your operating system. Sometimes, the most important thing you can do is upgrade to a version that can run the programs you need for success.

CHAPTER 12

I - IDENTIFY: HIDDEN ASSETS IN PLAIN SIGHT

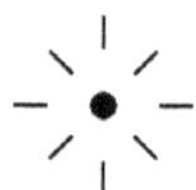

"The difference between stuck and unstuck isn't what you have, it's what you notice." ©

Feeling stuck often resembles being stranded in a desert, desperately scanning the horizon for resources you're convinced don't exist. Yet one of the most startling discoveries on the journey to clarity is that you're likely surrounded by untapped wealth, strengths you've dismissed, connections you've overlooked, and experiences whose true value remains hidden. This chapter will revolutionize your perception, training you to see the abundance that's been there all along.

Welcome to "I" in our method: learning to Identify the hidden resources that can transform scarcity into possibility.

This blindness to our resources isn't accidental; it's a natural consequence of focusing on what's missing rather than what's present. When we feel stuck, our attention automatically gravitates toward gaps, limitations, and things we lack. This scarcity mindset creates a perceptual filter that makes available resources invisible, even when they're sitting right in front of us.

The goal of this step isn't to ignore real constraints or pretend you have resources you don't possess. It's to develop the ability to see and leverage assets that have been hidden in plain sight, strengths, connections, experiences, and capabilities that could transform your situation if properly recognized and applied.

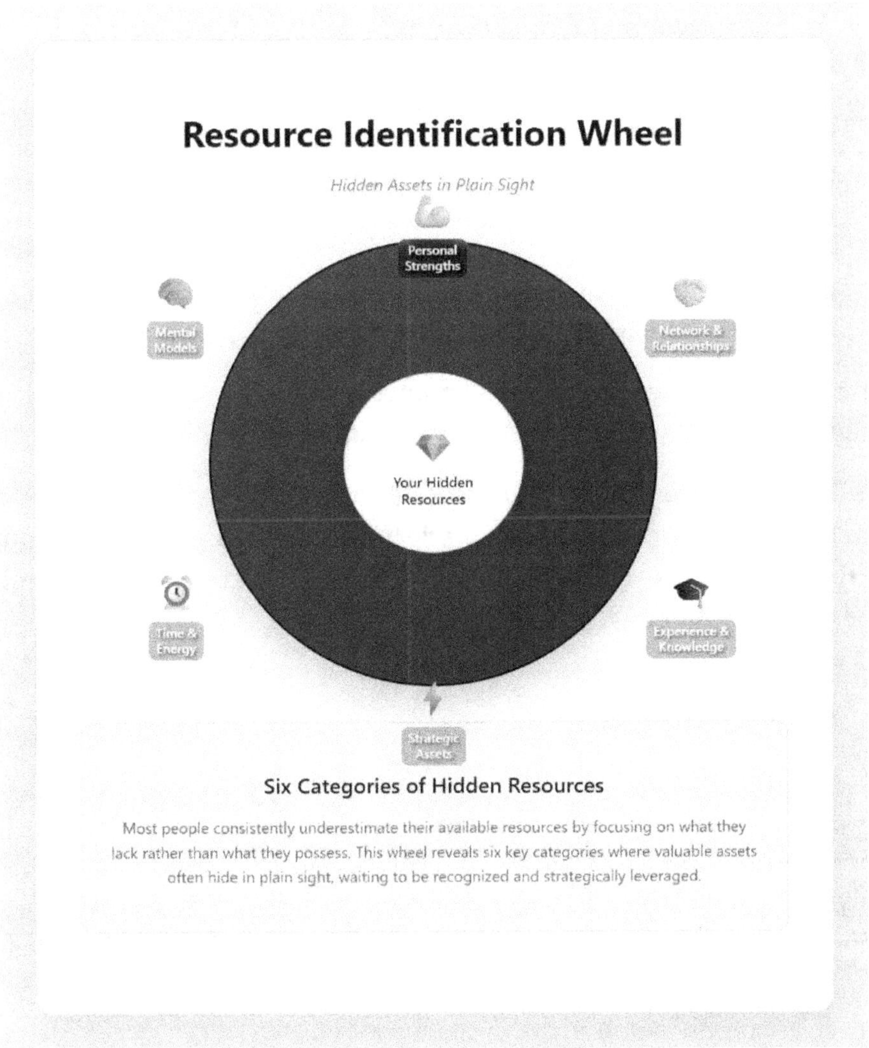
Resource Identification Wheel
Hidden Assets in Plain Sight
Personal Strengths
Mental Models
Network & Relationships
Your Hidden Resources
Time & Energy
Experience & Knowledge
Strategic Assets
Six Categories of Hidden Resources
Most people consistently underestimate their available resources by focusing on what they lack rather than what they possess. This wheel reveals six key categories where valuable assets often hide in plain sight, waiting to be recognized and strategically leveraged.

My Story: Discovering I Had Everything I Needed

When I first realized I needed to escape my toxic consulting situation, my immediate reaction was to focus on everything I lacked.

I didn't have influence within the firm. I didn't understand the political dynamics. I didn't have relationships with senior leadership. I didn't have experience navigating organizational conflicts. I didn't have a powerful coach who could advocate for me. I didn't have insider knowledge about how project assignments really worked.

This deficit thinking kept me paralyzed for months. Every potential solution seemed to require resources I didn't have access to. I felt trapped by the immediate situation and my apparent lack of tools for changing it.

The breakthrough came when I stopped cataloging what I lacked and started systematically inventorying what I actually had available.

This shift from scarcity thinking to asset recognition became a cornerstone of The CLARITY Code™: transformation often comes not from acquiring new resources, but from seeing and leveraging what you already possess.

The Hidden Strengths

The first category of overlooked resources was personal strengths I'd been taking for granted:

Analytical Thinking: I could break down complex situations into component parts and identify patterns. I'd been using this skill to analyze client problems, but I hadn't applied it to organizational dynamics or political situations within my own organization.

Relationship Building: Throughout my career, I've consistently built positive relationships with colleagues, clients, and managers. I'd been thinking of this as just "being friendly," but it was actually a sophisticated capability for creating trust and rapport with diverse personalities.

Strategic Communication: I could explain complex ideas clearly and persuasively. I regularly helped stakeholders understand complicated healthcare concepts in client settings and see new possibilities for their organizations.

Persistence: I had a track record of working through difficult challenges without giving up. The consulting situation felt different because it involved interpersonal dynamics rather than technical problems, but the underlying capability to persist through adversity was the same.

Learning Agility: I'd successfully transitioned between different roles, industries, and challenges throughout my career. I could quickly understand new environments and adapt my approach based on what I learned.

These weren't new capabilities I needed to develop—they were existing strengths that I'd never thought to apply to my current challenge.

The Available Network

The second category of hidden resources was relationships and connections I'd been overlooking:

Healthcare Industry Contacts: Through my previous roles, I have had relationships with people throughout the healthcare industry. While they couldn't directly help with my consulting firm politics, they provided perspective on my market value and alternative opportunities.

Business School Alumni: My MBA program connected me with people across various industries and consulting firms. I'd been thinking of these as social relationships rather than potential sources of advice and insight about navigating corporate environments.

Current Colleagues: I'd been so focused on the one person creating problems that I'd undervalued the relationships I was building with other team members, project managers, and consultants from different engagements.

Mentors and Former Managers: I had relationships with people who had successfully navigated similar challenges in their own careers. I'd been hesitant to reach out because I didn't want to seem like I was failing, but these were exactly the people who could provide guidance and perspective.

Family and Friends: While they couldn't solve my specific consulting challenge, they offered emotional support, outside perspective, and in some cases, professional networks I hadn't fully utilized.

Most importantly, I had potential access to senior partners within the firm itself—I just hadn't been strategic about building those relationships.

The Overlooked Experiences

The third category of hidden resources was experiences and knowledge I'd accumulated but wasn't leveraging:

Cross-Industry Perspective: My background spanning multiple healthcare sectors gave me insights that were valuable in consulting contexts, but I'd been underselling this experience rather than positioning it as a unique asset.

Crisis Management: I'd successfully handled various professional and personal crises over the years. The consulting situation felt different, but many of the same principles applied: staying calm under pressure, breaking problems into manageable pieces, seeking help when needed.

Educational Background: My combination of healthcare expertise and business education was relatively uncommon and valuable, but I'd been focusing on what I didn't know rather than leveraging what I did know.

Previous Success Stories: I'd successfully navigated other challenging work situations, difficult relationships, and complex projects. These experiences contained lessons and strategies I could adapt to my current circumstances.

Research Skills: Through my healthcare background and business education, I've developed strong capabilities for gathering and analyzing information. I could apply these same skills to understanding the consulting firm's culture, power dynamics, and informal networks.

The Strategic Assets

The fourth category of hidden resources was strategic advantages that I'd been completely blind to:

Industry Expertise: My deep industry knowledge was rare and valuable in a firm aligned with the healthcare consulting wing. Instead of seeing myself as just another consultant, I could position myself as someone who brought specialized expertise that few others possessed.

External Credibility: My reputation in the healthcare industry existed independently of the consulting firm's politics. This gave me leverage and options that someone without external credibility wouldn't have.

Recent MBA: My advanced degree is current and from a respected program. This provided credibility and network access that I hadn't fully utilized.

Project Results: Despite the political challenges, I was actually delivering strong results for clients. I had objective evidence of my value that transcended the interpersonal conflicts.

Time and Energy: While the situation was emotionally draining, I was young, energetic, and had the capacity to invest significant effort in solving the challenge. This was an asset that not everyone in similar situations possessed.

The Resource Integration Strategy

Once I identified these overlooked resources, I wondered how to integrate them into a strategic approach to my situation.

I realized I could combine my analytical thinking with my research skills to systematically understand the firm's power dynamics rather than just reacting emotionally to daily frustrations.

I could leverage my relationship-building capabilities to strategically network with senior partners rather than just hoping someone would notice my good work.

I could use my strategic communication skills to position my industry expertise as a valuable asset rather than just expecting people to recognize its value automatically.

I could apply my persistence and learning agility to navigate the political challenges with the same systematic approach I used for technical consulting problems.

Most importantly, I could combine my external credibility with my internal relationship-building to create the coaching transition strategy that ultimately solved my immediate problem while building capabilities for future challenges.

The Mindset Shift

The most profound change wasn't discovering specific resources; it was shifting from a scarcity mindset that focused on what I lacked to an abundance mindset that recognized what I already had available.

This shift changed not just how I approached the consulting situation, but how I've approached every challenge since then. Instead of immediately cataloging what I'm missing, I now start by inventorying what I already have access to.

This doesn't mean ignoring real constraints or pretending limitations don't exist. It means ensuring that I'm building from a foundation of available resources rather than starting from a position of perceived deficit.

In The **CLARITY Code™**, identifying hidden resources isn't about wishful thinking; it's about developing the perceptual skills to see abundance where you previously saw only scarcity.

The Principle: Most People Have More Resources Than They Realize

My experience illustrates a fundamental truth about resources: the primary constraint is usually not availability but recognition and utilization.

Here's why people consistently underestimate their available resources:

1. Familiarity Breeds Blindness

We tend to discount things that come naturally to us or that we've always had access to. Skills that feel easy seem less valuable, relationships that developed organically seem less strategic, and experiences that feel "normal" seem less significant.

2. Context Dependency

Resources that were valuable in one context may seem irrelevant in another, even when they could be adapted or transferred. Professional skills might not seem applicable to personal challenges, or technical capabilities might not seem relevant to interpersonal situations.

3. Narrow Definitions

People often have restrictive definitions of what counts as a "resource." They focus on formal qualifications, official positions, or financial assets while overlooking intangible assets like relationships, experiences, personal qualities, and accumulated knowledge.

4. Comparison Trap

People focus on relative disadvantages while missing absolute advantages when comparing themselves to others. They notice what others have that they lack while overlooking what they have that others might lack.

5. Problem-Focused Attention

When stuck, people naturally focus on what's wrong or missing rather than what's working or available. This problem-focused attention creates a perceptual filter that makes assets invisible while amplifying deficits.

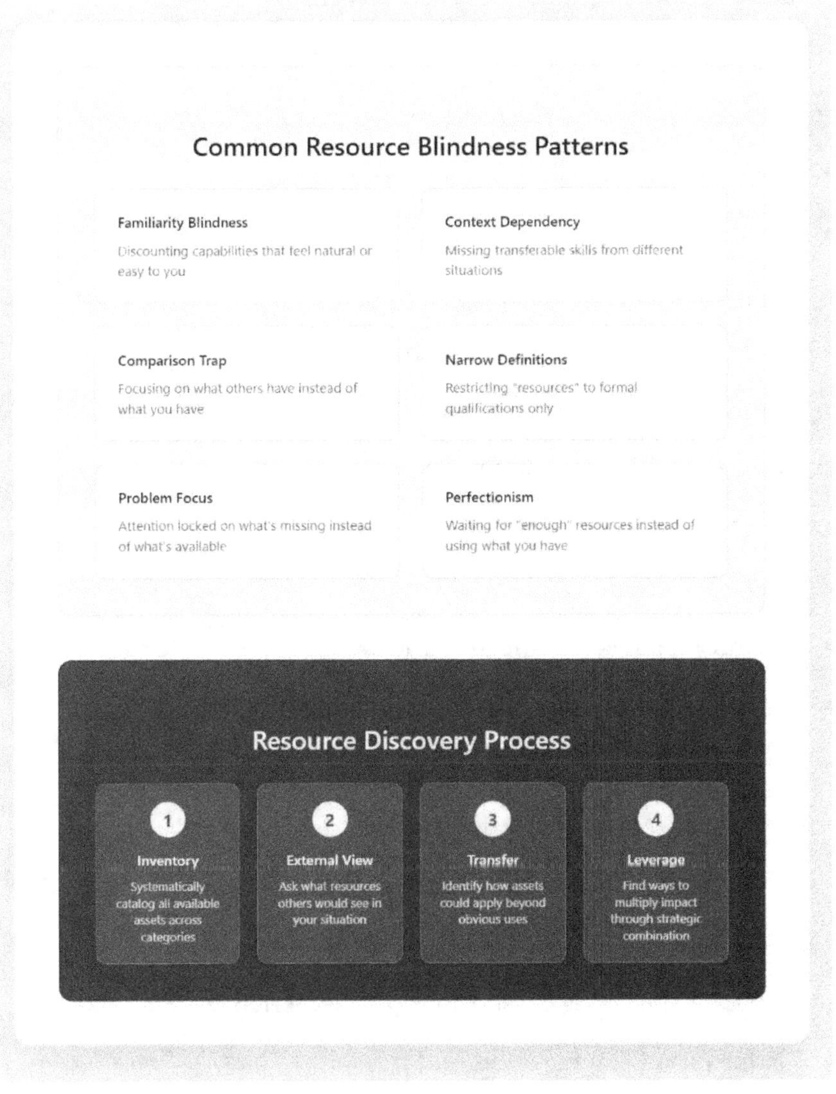

The Process: Systematic Resource Inventory and Leverage

Based on my experience helping people discover and utilize their hidden resources, here's how to approach this step systematically:

1. Conduct a Comprehensive Asset Inventory

Create categories and systematically identify resources in each area:

Personal Strengths and Capabilities:

- Natural talents and developed skills
- Knowledge and expertise (formal and informal)
- Personal qualities and characteristics
- Learning abilities and adaptability
- Physical and mental health assets

Relationship and Network Assets:

- Professional contacts and colleagues
- Personal friends and family members
- Mentors, advisors, and role models
- Alum networks and community connections
- Industry associations and group memberships

Experience and Knowledge Resources:

- Previous successes and breakthrough moments
- Lessons learned from past challenges
- Cross-industry or cross-functional experience
- Educational background and training
- Life experiences that built resilience or perspective

Tangible and Strategic Assets:

- Financial resources (even modest savings)

- Time and energy availability

- Location and access advantages

- Technology and tools at your disposal

- Credentials, certifications, and formal qualifications

2. Apply the "Outside Observer" Perspective

Imagine you're helping a friend in your exact situation. What resources would you encourage them to leverage? What assets would seem obvious to you that they might be overlooking?

This perspective helps bypass the blind spots that come from being too close to your own situation.

3. Use the "Successful Person" Framework

Think of someone who has successfully navigated a challenge similar to yours. What resources did they have available? Now look at your own asset inventory. Which of those same types of resources do you already possess but haven't been utilizing?

4. Question Your Assumptions About Requirements

Challenge beliefs about what resources are "necessary" for progress:

- What do you think you need that you might not actually need?

- Are there alternative approaches that would require different resources you don't have?

- What would someone with your exact resources but a different mindset be able to achieve?

5. Look for Transferable Applications

Examine each asset for potential applications beyond its obvious use:

- How could professional skills apply to personal challenges?

- How could personal strengths transfer to professional situations?

- What could you adapt from one area of life to another?

- How could past experience in different contexts inform current challenges?

6. Identify Amplification Opportunities

Look for ways to multiply the impact of available resources:

- Which relationships could introduce you to other valuable connections?

- How could small financial resources be leveraged into larger opportunities?

- What skills could be combined to create unique value propositions?

- How could your time and energy be invested for maximum strategic return?

Common Resource Blindness Patterns

"I Don't Have Any Special Skills"

This usually means you're discounting capabilities that feel natural or easy to you. The things that come naturally often represent your greatest strengths.

Try asking: "What do people regularly ask for my help with?" or "What seems easy to me but difficult for others?"

"My Network Isn't Powerful Enough"

This assumes you need connections to extremely influential people, when often you need connections to the right people for your specific situation.

Map your network based on relevance to your current challenge rather than general influence or status.

"I Don't Have Enough Experience"

This overlooks transferable lessons from different contexts and undervalues the unique perspective that comes from your particular combination of experiences.

Look for patterns and principles from your past experiences that could apply to new situations.

"I Can't Afford to Make Changes"

This often comes from overestimating the financial requirements for progress and underestimating creative alternatives.

Research the actual costs of change and explore low-cost or no-cost approaches to moving forward.

"I Don't Know the Right People"

This assumes you need to know specific individuals rather than having access to categories of people who could provide guidance, support, or opportunities.

Focus on the types of people who could be helpful, then look for ways to connect with people in those categories through your existing network.

Integration with Other CLARITY Steps

Resource identification becomes most powerful when integrated with the other elements of The CLARITY Code™:

Confronting Reality (C) helps you see which resources you actually have versus which ones you think you should have.

Locating Destination (L) clarifies which resources are most relevant to your specific goals.

Analyzing Obstacles (A) reveals which resources could address your real barriers versus surface-level problems.

Reframing Beliefs (R) transforms limiting beliefs about necessary or available resources.

Taking Action (T) provides concrete ways to leverage your identified resources strategically.

Yielding Momentum (Y) ensures you continue building and expanding your resource base over time.

Why This Step Is Essential for Sustainable Progress

Resource identification is crucial because it:

1. Builds Confidence from Reality

When you clearly see what you have available, confidence comes from an accurate assessment rather than false optimism. This reality-based confidence is more stable and sustainable.

2. Enables Strategic Thinking

You can't develop effective strategies without accurate knowledge of your available assets. Resource blindness leads to either overly conservative approaches (because you underestimate your capabilities) or unrealistic plans (because you don't know what you actually have to work with).

3. Prevents Unnecessary Delays

Many people postpone taking action because they believe they need resources they don't have or cannot work around. Recognizing available assets eliminates artificial barriers to progress.

4. Creates Leverage Points

Small resources applied strategically often produce disproportionate results. However, you can only create leverage when you clearly see what you have available to work with.

5. Builds Resourcefulness

Learning to see and utilize available assets develops the skill of resourcefulness—the ability to make the most of whatever situation you find yourself in.

The Transformation Impact

In my consulting situation, the shift from focusing on what I lacked to leveraging what I had available completely changed my experience and outcomes.

Instead of feeling powerless and trapped, I felt capable and strategic. Instead of waiting for external circumstances to change, I took systematic action using available resources. Instead of viewing the situation as something happening to me, I saw it as a challenge I had the tools to address.

Most importantly, the resource identification process revealed that I had been much more capable and well-equipped than I'd realized. This recognition solved my immediate problem and fundamentally changed how I approach any challenging situation.

The resources had been there all along. I just needed to develop the eyes to see them and the wisdom to use them strategically.

That's the power of identifying hidden assets: it doesn't change what you have available—it changes what you can see and do with what you've always had.

The abundance was always there. You just needed to learn how to recognize it.

CHAPTER 13

T - TAKE ACTION: FROM ANALYSIS TO IMPLEMENTATION

"Strategy without action is just expensive planning. Action without strategy is just expensive hope." ©

Clarity without action is sophisticated procrastination. You can perfectly understand your situation, crystallize your vision, decode your obstacles, and transform your thinking, but until you move strategically in the physical world, nothing actually changes. The gulf between insight and impact is bridged by one element: intelligent action that leverages everything you've discovered about your situation.

This chapter is dedicated to "T": how to Take strategic action that transforms understanding into unstoppable momentum.

The problem isn't usually a lack of motivation. After working through the first five steps of The CLARITY Code™, most people feel energized and ready to move forward. The problem is that they approach action the same way they've always approached it: through willpower, general effort, and hoping that working harder will somehow produce different results.

Strategic action is fundamentally different. It's about applying concentrated effort to specific leverage points that can create disproportionate results. It's about taking the intelligence you've gathered through the CLARITY process and translating it into moves that actually change your situation.

My Story: The Coaching Gambit

After months of spinning my wheels in the toxic consulting situation, I finally had the clarity I needed to take strategic action. I understood the real obstacles (organizational politics and power dynamics), I'd reframed my beliefs (from victim to student), and I'd identified my resources (industry expertise, relationship-building skills, and external credibility).

But knowing what needed to be done and actually doing it effectively are two completely different challenges.

My first attempts at action were scattered and ineffective. I tried networking with various partners, documenting my client successes more systematically, and building better relationships with my immediate colleagues. These weren't bad ideas, but they weren't strategic enough to create meaningful change in my situation.

The breakthrough came when I stopped thinking about individual actions and started thinking about systematic leverage.

What single move could address multiple obstacles simultaneously while utilizing my strongest resources?

That question led to what I now call "the coaching gambit," a strategic action that seemed risky but was precisely calculated to create the outcome I needed.

The Strategic Design

Here's how the coaching gambit was designed to work:

The Core Move: Request a coaching change, positioning it as a way better to leverage my healthcare expertise for the firm's benefit.

Surface Level: This looked like a simple administrative request to work with someone who could better guide my career development in healthcare consulting.

Strategic Level: This was actually a sophisticated political maneuver designed to accomplish multiple objectives simultaneously:

1. **Extract me from the toxic situation** without having to prove wrongdoing or ask for rescue

2. **Position my healthcare expertise as valuable** rather than letting it be marginalized

3. **Connect me with someone who has actual influence** in my business vertical

4. **Create a legitimate reason to network with senior partners** as part of the coaching selection process

5. **Demonstrate strategic thinking and initiative** rather than just enduring the situation passively

6. **Maintain relationships** with current colleagues while creating distance from the problematic dynamic

The Execution: I scheduled a meeting with my current coach and explained that I wanted to maximize my contribution to the firm's healthcare practice. I'd been reflecting on how to utilize my industry background best, and I thought working with a coach specializing in healthcare consulting would help me be more effective.

The Frame: This wasn't about escaping a problem but optimizing my value to the organization.

This framing was crucial because it positioned the request as being in the firm's interest rather than just my personal preference. It also demonstrated the kind of strategic thinking that consulting firms value in their employees.

Why This Action Was Strategic

The coaching gambit succeeded because it was designed according to strategic action principles that I've since applied to every challenging situation:

1. It Addressed Root Causes, Not Just Symptoms

Instead of trying to improve my current situation (symptom-level action), the coaching change addressed the underlying structural problem: I was trapped in a dynamic with someone who had incentives to undermine my success.

2. It Leveraged My Strongest Resources

The move utilized my healthcare expertise (positioning it as valuable), my relationship-building skills (networking with potential coaches), and my strategic communication abilities (framing the request effectively).

3. It Aligned With System Incentives

Rather than fighting against the firm's culture, the coaching change worked within it. The firm wanted healthcare expertise and valued strategic thinking; my request demonstrated both.

4. It Created Multiple Pathways to Success

Even if the coaching change had been denied, the process would have accomplished several beneficial outcomes: increased visibility with senior partners, positioning of my expertise, and demonstration of strategic initiative.

5. It Minimized Downside Risk

The request was reasonable and professionally positioned. Even in the worst-case scenario, it would have been considered an appropriate ambition rather than problematic behavior.

6. It Established New Patterns

Instead of waiting for circumstances to change, I was taking strategic initiative to shape my situation. This shift from reactive to proactive set the tone for everything that followed.

The Results

The coaching gambit succeeded beyond my expectations.

Within two weeks, I was working with a senior leader who specialized in my expertise. Within a month, I was transitioning to a new project where my expertise was valued and my contributions were recognized. Within six months, I received the kind of client feedback and project assignments I'd hoped for since I started at the firm.

However, the most important result wasn't the immediate situation improvement; I developed a systematic approach to strategic action through this experience.

I learned that effective action isn't about working harder or trying more things. It's about identifying leverage points where small moves can create large changes, then executing those moves with precision and strategic thinking.

This became a cornerstone of The CLARITY Code™: strategic action multiplies the impact of effort by applying it to the right targets in the right way at the right time.

Strategic Action Design

From Analysis to High-Impact Implementation

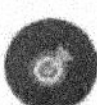 ## Define Strategic Objectives

Immediate Goals

? What specific changes do you need in your situation?

? What would success look like in 30-90 days?

? Which outcomes are absolutely critical?

Systemic Changes

? What underlying patterns need to shift?

? How do you want to be perceived differently?

? What relationships need strengthening?

 ## Identify Leverage Points

Key Decisions

? Who makes the decisions that affect your situation?

? What influences their decision-making process?

? When are these decisions typically made?

Critical Relationships

? Which relationships are most crucial to your success?

? Who has influence over key stakeholders?

? What would change if these relationships improved?

 ## Design Integrated Actions

Multi-Objective Moves

? How could one action address multiple obstacles?

? What would demonstrate several strengths simultaneously?

? Which moves create value for multiple stakeholders?

System Alignment

? What does the system reward or incentivize?

? How can you work with existing patterns?

? What approach would benefit others while helping you?

The Principle: How Strategic Action Differs from General Effort

My coaching gambit illustrates the fundamental difference between strategic action and the kind of general effort that most people apply when they're trying to change their situation.

Here's how strategic action creates disproportionate results:

1. Leverage Over Volume

Strategic action focuses on finding points where small efforts can create large changes, rather than assuming that more effort automatically leads to better results.

In complex systems—whether organizational, personal, or interpersonal—there are usually specific points where pressure applied correctly can shift the entire dynamic. Strategic action is about finding and utilizing these leverage points.

2. Integration Over Isolation

Strategic action is designed to address multiple challenges simultaneously rather than tackling problems one at a time.

My coaching change solved the toxic relationship problem, effectively positioned my expertise, connected me with influential people, and demonstrated strategic thinking through a single coordinated move.

3. System Alignment Over System Fighting

Strategic action works with the natural incentives and patterns of the system you're operating within, rather than trying to force the system to operate differently.

Instead of trying to make organizational politics disappear, I learned to navigate them effectively. Instead of fighting the firm's culture, I learned to succeed within it.

4. Sustainable Change Over Temporary Results

Strategic action creates changes that become self-reinforcing rather than requiring constant effort to maintain.

Once, I was working with an influential coach on projects that valued my expertise, and the new dynamic maintained itself. I didn't have to keep fighting for recognition—the system was now structured to provide it naturally.

5. Measured Risk Over Reckless Courage

Strategic action involves calculated risks based on careful analysis rather than either playing it safe or making desperate moves.

The coaching request required courage, but it was courage informed by a systematic understanding of the risks, potential outcomes, and alternative approaches.

The Process: Designing and Executing Strategic Action

Based on my experience helping people translate clarity into effective action, here's how to approach this step systematically:

1. Define Your Strategic Objectives

Before choosing specific actions, be clear about what you're trying to accomplish at multiple levels:

Immediate Objectives: What specific changes do you need in your situation?

Systemic Objectives: What underlying patterns or dynamics need to shift?

Development Objectives: What capabilities do you want to build through this process? **Relationship Objectives**: How do you want to affect your relationships with key people? **Positioning Objectives**: How do you want to be perceived after taking action?

2. Identify Leverage Points

Look for places where small actions could create large changes:

- What key decisions affect your situation, and who makes them?

- What relationships are most crucial to your success?

- What perceptions about you or your situation most need to change?

- What resources or capabilities could you develop that would change everything?

- What single change would make the biggest difference in your day-to-day experience?

3. Design Integrated Actions

Look for moves that can accomplish multiple objectives simultaneously:

- How could one action address several different obstacles?

- What would allow you to demonstrate multiple strengths at once?

- How could you build relationships while also showcasing capabilities?

- What would position you well regardless of the specific outcome?

4. Align With System Incentives

Ensure your actions work with the natural patterns of your environment rather than against them:

- What does the system reward, and how can your actions demonstrate those qualities?

- Who are the key stakeholders, and how can your moves benefit them?

- What are the informal rules of success, and how can you operate within them?

- How can you make helping you also help others achieve their goals?

5. Plan for Multiple Scenarios

Strategic action includes contingency planning for different possible outcomes:

- What's your approach if everything goes better than expected?

- What's your backup plan if your primary approach doesn't work?

- How will you adjust if you encounter unexpected obstacles?

- What would you do if you achieve partial but not complete success?

6. Execute with Precision

Implementation matters as much as strategy:

- What's the optimal timing for your action?

- How will you communicate your intentions and reasoning?

- Who needs to be involved or informed?

- What follow-up actions will be required?

- How will you measure progress and adjust course if needed?

Implementation Readiness Checklist

- ☐ Clear understanding of desired outcomes
- ☐ Identified leverage points and key relationships
- ☐ Resources and capabilities assessed
- ☐ Timing and sequence planned
- ☐ Stakeholder impact considered
- ☐ Contingency plans developed
- ☐ Success metrics defined
- ☐ Follow-up actions planned

Common Strategic Action Mistakes

Taking Action Too Early

Many people rush into action before they've done sufficient analysis and planning. This usually leads to effort being applied to the wrong targets or in ineffective ways.

Ensure you've worked through the first five steps of The CLARITY Code™ before moving to action. Strategic action is only strategic when a clear understanding of your situation, goals, obstacles, beliefs, and resources informs it.

Confusing Motion with Progress

Activity isn't automatically productive. Taking lots of action can actually be counterproductive if it's not strategically designed.

Focus on quality over quantity. One well-designed strategic move often accomplishes more than dozens of random activities.

Underestimating Implementation Requirements

Good strategies can fail due to poor execution. Strategic action requires attention to timing, communication, relationship management, and follow-through.

Plan the implementation process as carefully as you plan the strategy itself.

Avoiding Calculated Risks

Strategic action usually involves some level of risk or discomfort. People who only take actions that feel completely safe rarely create meaningful change.

The goal isn't to eliminate risk but to take calculated risks based on careful analysis of potential outcomes and backup plans.

Neglecting the Human Element

Strategies that look good on paper can fail if they don't account for human psychology, relationships, and political dynamics.

Always consider how your actions will be perceived and how they might affect key relationships.

Integration with Previous CLARITY Steps

Strategic action becomes most effective when it builds on the foundation created by the previous steps:

Your confrontation of reality (C) ensures your actions address the actual situation rather than the situation you wish existed.

Your destination clarity (L) ensures your actions move you toward specific goals rather than just away from current problems.

Your obstacle analysis (A) ensures your actions address root causes rather than just surface symptoms.

Your belief transformation (R) ensures your actions are based on empowering assumptions about what's possible.

Your resource identification (I) ensures your actions leverage what you actually have available rather than what you wish you had.

The strategic action step (T) transforms all of this preparation into concrete moves that create real change in your situation.

Why This Step Is Essential for Results

Analysis without action is just sophisticated procrastination. You can gain tremendous clarity about your situation, but until you take strategic action based on that clarity, nothing actually changes.

Strategic action is also essential for learning. You can think through situations extensively, but never really know what will work until you test your understanding through real-world implementation.

Most importantly, strategic action builds your capabilities and confidence to handle future challenges. Each time you successfully design and execute strategic moves, you develop better instincts for navigating complex situations.

In my consulting experience, everything changed when I moved from reactive coping to strategic action. The coaching gambit wasn't just a successful tactic—it was a template for approaching any situation where I needed to create change through intelligent action rather than force or luck.

That's the power of strategic action: it converts clarity into results, insights into outcomes, and understanding into transformation.

The intelligence you've gathered through the CLARITY process is only valuable if you apply it systematically to change your actual situation.

Strategy without action is just planning. Action without strategy is just hope.

Strategic action is where clarity becomes change.

CHAPTER 14

Y - YIELD: BUILDING SUSTAINABLE MOMENTUM

"Impactful clarity isn't about solving your current problem—it's building your capacity to solve whatever problems come next." ©

The ultimate test of any transformation isn't the initial breakthrough; it's what happens six months later. Do you maintain your progress or gradually drift back toward familiar patterns? Most people experience what I call "breakthrough and breakdown": moments of significant progress followed by slow regression to previous states.

The final element of The CLARITY Code™ addresses this crucial challenge: how to "Y"ield sustainable momentum that doesn't just solve your current problem, but fundamentally upgrades your capacity to handle whatever complex challenges arise next.

This approach leads to what I call "breakthrough and breakdown," periods of significant progress followed by gradual regression back toward previous patterns. The initial success creates temporary momentum, but without systematic reinforcement, the old dynamics eventually reassert themselves.

True transformation requires more than solving immediate problems. It requires building the systems, habits, relationships, and capabilities that ensure your progress continues and compounds over time.

My Story: Beyond the Consulting Victory

The coaching gambit succeeded brilliantly. Within months, I worked on challenging projects, received positive client feedback, and built valuable relationships with key leaders. My immediate problem was solved, and my career trajectory had fundamentally shifted.

But the most important learning came from what happened after the initial success.

I could have treated the coaching change as a one-time fix, a clever move that solved my immediate problem. If I'd done that, I probably would have continued succeeding in the short term but eventually encountered similar challenges when faced with new organizational dynamics or political situations.

Instead, I used the success as a foundation for building systematic capabilities that would serve me in any complex professional situation I might encounter in the future.

This shift from solving problems to building capabilities became the essence of the "Yield" step in The CLARITY Code™.

The Systematic Approach

Here's how I converted the tactical success into sustainable momentum:

1. Documented the Process

Instead of just celebrating the outcome, I systematically analyzed what had made the strategy successful:

- What beliefs and mental models had enabled strategic thinking?

- What analytical frameworks have helped me understand the situation accurately?

- What relationship-building approaches had been most effective?

- What communication strategies had positioned my request optimally?

- What timing and execution factors had been crucial?

This documentation served two purposes: it helped me understand the transferable principles behind the success and created a reference guide for applying similar thinking to future challenges.

2. Expanded the Skill Set

The coaching situation revealed that navigating organizational politics was a crucial professional capability I'd lacked. Instead of just being grateful that I'd stumbled through it successfully, I made systematic development of these skills a priority:

I started reading about organizational behavior and power dynamics. I sought out mentors who could teach me about relationship building and influence. I began observing successful colleagues more systematically to understand their strategic thinking patterns.

3. Built Strategic Relationships

The coaching change had connected me with influential people within the firm, but I didn't just maintain those relationships passively. I approached relationship building as a systematic capability to develop:

I learned how to provide value to senior colleagues beyond just doing good project work. I developed skills for staying visible and connected without being pushy or political. I created systems for maintaining relationships even when I wasn't working directly with people.

4. Created Feedback Loops

I established regular check-ins with my new coach and other trusted colleagues to ensure I continued developing strategically rather than just executing tasks effectively. These conversations helped me stay aware of how my actions were being perceived and how my reputation was evolving within the firm.

5. Applied the Framework to New Challenges

Most importantly, I began using the analytical and strategic thinking approach that had solved the coaching situation to address other professional and personal challenges. Each new application strengthened the underlying capabilities while proving the approach was genuinely transferable.

The Compound Effect

The difference between treating success as an endpoint versus building sustainable momentum became clear over the following years.

Instead of just being someone who had solved one difficult situation, I became someone who had systematic approaches for navigating any complex challenge. Instead of having one good outcome, I developed capabilities that created ongoing advantages in every professional situation I encountered.

The consulting experience had taught me more than how to handle toxic colleagues or navigate organizational politics. It had taught me how to approach any stuck situation with strategic thinking, systematic analysis, and confidence in my ability to create solutions.

This evolution from tactical success to strategic capability is what sustainable momentum looks like: progress that creates the foundation for continued progress rather than just solving immediate problems.

In The CLARITY Code™, yielding momentum isn't about maintaining specific outcomes but building the systems and capabilities that make continued success inevitable.

The Principle: How Momentum Becomes Self-Reinforcing

My experience illustrates a fundamental truth about sustainable change: momentum isn't just about continuing to move forward; it's about creating conditions where progress becomes easier and more natural over time.

Here's how sustainable momentum actually works:

1. Capabilities Compound

Each challenge you navigate strategically builds skills and knowledge that make future challenges easier to handle. You're not just solving problems; you're developing problem-solving capabilities that apply to all categories of situations.

2. Confidence Builds on Evidence

Success based on systematic thinking creates a different kind of confidence than success based on luck or external circumstances. You can replicate and adapt the approach for new situations when you know why something worked.

3. Relationships Create Exponential Opportunities

Strategic relationship building creates networks that provide ongoing access to information, opportunities, and support. These relationships often become more valuable over time as people advance in their own careers.

4. Reputation Generates Momentum

When people see you as someone who handles challenges effectively, they're more likely to include you in opportunities, seek your input on decisions, and support your initiatives. Success creates a reputation that makes future success more likely.

5. Systems Reduce Friction

When you build effective systems for analyzing situations, making decisions, and taking action, these systems reduce the energy required for future challenges. You spend less time figuring out how to approach problems and more time executing solutions.

6. Perspective Transforms Challenges

When you've successfully navigated difficult situations before, new challenges feel less overwhelming and more manageable. Your expanded perspective helps you see opportunities where others see only obstacles.

The Process: Building Systems for Sustainable Momentum

Based on my experience helping people convert breakthrough moments into lasting transformation, here's how to approach this step systematically:

1. Capture the Learning

Immediately after any significant success, conduct a systematic learning analysis:

What Worked:

- Which specific actions created the best results?

- What thinking patterns or mental models were most helpful?

- Which relationships or resources were most crucial?

- What timing or environmental factors contributed to success?

What You Learned:

- What did you discover about yourself that you didn't know before?

- What assumptions were proven correct or incorrect?

- What skills did you develop through the process?

- What would you do differently if facing a similar situation again?

What's Transferable:

- Which elements of your approach could apply to other types of challenges?

- What principles could guide future decision-making?

- What systems or processes could be replicated?

- Which relationship-building strategies could be used in different contexts?

2. Identify Capability Gaps

Use your success to illuminate areas for continued development:

- What skills would have made the process easier or more effective?

- What knowledge would have helped you recognize opportunities sooner?

- What relationships would have provided additional options or support?

- What systems would have reduced stress or uncertainty during the process?

3. Build Systematic Development Plans

Convert insights into concrete development strategies:

Skill Development: Create specific plans for building capabilities that would make future challenges easier to navigate.

Knowledge Acquisition: Identify information, frameworks, or expertise that would expand your strategic thinking abilities.

Relationship Building: Develop systematic approaches for building and maintaining the kinds of relationships that provide ongoing value.

System Creation: Build processes, habits, and tools that make effective decision-making and action-taking more automatic.

4. Create Feedback Mechanisms

Establish systems for ongoing assessment and course correction:

- Regular check-ins with mentors or advisors who can provide an outside perspective

- Metrics or indicators that help you track progress on development goals

- Peer relationships that provide honest feedback about your growth

- Self-reflection practices that help you stay aware of patterns and progress

5. Apply Learning to New Challenges

Actively look for opportunities to practice and expand your capabilities:

- Volunteer for projects or roles that require the skills you're developing

- Seek out challenges that will test and strengthen your strategic thinking

- Mentor others facing similar situations to reinforce your own learning

- Share your approaches with colleagues to get feedback and improve your frameworks

6. Document and Refine Your Approach

Create systems for capturing and improving your methodologies:

- Write down your frameworks and decision-making processes

- Keep records of what works and what doesn't in different contexts

- Regularly update your approaches based on new experiences and learning

- Share your methods with others to test their effectiveness and get input for improvement

Common Momentum-Killing Mistakes

Treating Success as Luck

When people attribute their success to external factors rather than systematic approaches, they miss opportunities to build repeatable capabilities.

Focus on understanding what you did that contributed to the outcome, even when external factors also played a role.

Moving On Too Quickly

The period immediately after success is often the best time for learning and building momentum. People who rush to the next challenge miss opportunities to consolidate their gains.

Build reflection and analysis time into your approach to change. The learning phase is as important as the action phase.

Neglecting Relationship Maintenance

Many people invest significant effort in building relationships during challenging periods but neglect those relationships once the immediate need passes.

Treat relationship building as an ongoing investment rather than a tactical necessity. The strongest networks are built during calm periods, not just during crises.

Failing to Update Mental Models

Sometimes people achieve success despite incorrect beliefs about how change works. If they don't update their mental models, they may struggle when facing new types of challenges.

Regularly examine and update your beliefs about success based on your experiences.

Assuming the Work Is Done

Sustainable change requires ongoing attention and reinforcement. People who think one success means they've "figured it out" often slide back toward previous patterns.

View success as the beginning of a new level of effectiveness rather than the end of the change process.

Integration with the Complete CLARITY System

The Yield step brings the entire CLARITY Code™ full circle by ensuring that each application of the framework strengthens your ability to apply it in the future:

Your systematic approach to **Confronting reality** becomes more refined with each application.

Your skill at **Locating destinations** becomes more precise as you learn what kinds of goals actually motivate and fulfill you.

Your ability to **Analyze obstacles** becomes more sophisticated as you recognize patterns across different situations.

Your capacity for **Reframing beliefs** becomes more natural as you prove to yourself that empowering perspectives create better outcomes.

Your talent for **Identifying resources** becomes more automatic as you develop confidence in your own capabilities and network.

Your effectiveness at **Taking action** becomes more strategic as you build experience with what actually works in complex situations.

And your commitment to **Yielding momentum** becomes the foundation that makes every other step more powerful over time.

Why This Step Is Essential for Lasting Transformation

Without systematic momentum building, even the most successful applications of The CLARITY Code™ remain isolated victories rather than transformational capabilities.

The goal isn't just to solve your current stuck point; it's to develop the systematic approaches that ensure you never stay stuck for long in any situation.

The goal isn't just to achieve your current goal; it's to build the capabilities that make achieving meaningful goals a reliable pattern rather than an occasional breakthrough.

The goal isn't just to navigate your current challenge—it's to develop the confidence and competence that make you someone who can handle whatever complex situations life presents.

In my consulting experience, the coaching gambit was important, but the systems thinking and relationship-building capabilities I developed from that experience have been invaluable throughout my entire career. Every complex situation I've faced since then has been easier to navigate because of the foundations I built during and after that initial challenge.

That's the power of yielding sustainable momentum: it converts isolated successes into systematic capabilities, temporary improvements into lasting transformation, and breakthrough moments into breakthrough patterns.

The real victory isn't solving your current problem; it's building your capacity to solve whatever problems come next.

CHAPTER 15

THE ULTIMATE TEST CASE

" Real-world problems don't respect the boundaries you put around them." ©

When my wife came home frustrated about her student loan situation, I had no idea I was about to put my newly formalized CLARITY Code™ to its biggest test.

Up until this point, my framework had been applied to relatively straightforward situations: my consulting crisis, helping friends with career transitions, and guiding colleagues through workplace challenges. These were complex problems, but they involved clear stakeholders, understandable systems, and manageable timelines.

My wife was facing something entirely different: a multi-layered crisis involving federal loan forgiveness programs, changing political administrations, organizational classifications, personal fulfillment, financial pressure, and career identity—all interconnected in ways that made simple solutions impossible.

More importantly, this wasn't just about testing whether my method worked. This was about the person I cared most about, facing a situation that could affect our financial future and her professional happiness for years to come.

If The CLARITY Code™ was really as powerful as I believed it to be, it needed to work here, with the highest stakes I'd ever encountered.

The Crisis Unfolds

My wife's situation was a perfect storm of bureaucratic complexity and personal anguish.

She had spent years working in the public and non-profit sector specifically to qualify for the Public Service Loan Forgiveness (PSLF) program. After making 120 monthly payments while working for qualifying organizations, her substantial student loan debt would be completely forgiven. She was close, so close, to reaching that magical number of payments.

Then she discovered that her current organization, an organization she absolutely loved working for, was classified as a 501(c)(4) rather than a 501(c)(3). This seemingly minor difference in non-profit classification, for that specific organization, meant that her years of payments at this organization wouldn't count toward PSLF eligibility.

The discovery was devastating. Her beloved organization couldn't change its legal entity structure and classification—they had chosen that structure for valid business reasons. This meant she would need to leave the organization she loved to work elsewhere and complete her PSLF requirements, with no guarantee she could ever return.

With political winds shifting in Washington and a new federal administration coming in that was publicly hostile to student loan forgiveness programs, the window for qualifying might be closing rapidly.

She was facing an impossible choice: stay at an organization she loved but lose years of progress toward loan forgiveness, or find a new job at a qualifying organization but potentially give up forever the work she was passionate about, all while racing against potential policy changes that could eliminate the program entirely.

When she tried to discuss potential solutions with her current employer's leadership team, their response was essentially: "We understand this is unfortunate for you personally, but there's nothing we can do about our organizational classification."

She came home that evening more discouraged than I'd ever seen her.

"I feel completely trapped," she said. "No matter what I choose, I lose something important. And I'm running out of time to make any choice at all."

Applying the Method Unconsciously

As she described her situation, I found myself naturally moving through The CLARITY Code™ framework, though I didn't tell her that's what I was doing. I wanted to test whether the method worked when applied organically rather than formally.

C - Confront: Getting Clear About Reality

My first instinct was to help her see the situation clearly, without the emotional overwhelm that was clouding her thinking.

"Let's make sure we understand exactly what we're dealing with," I said. "Walk me through the timeline and the key facts."

As she laid out the details, several important realities became clear:

- She had already made significant progress toward loan forgiveness through her previous positions, so she wasn't starting from zero

- The political timeline was compressed, but not impossible; the new administration wouldn't take office for several months

- Her current organization genuinely valued her work, even if they couldn't solve the classification issue

- She had maintained strong relationships and a reputation in her industry

- Her field was relatively small and network-driven, which could be either an advantage or a constraint

- Leaving temporarily didn't necessarily mean permanently giving up on the work she loved

The most important reality that emerged was that she wasn't just dealing with a loan forgiveness problem, she was dealing with a career trajectory challenge that required strategic thinking across multiple phases.

L - Locate: Defining Success Precisely

Instead of letting her stay stuck in "I need to solve this loan problem," I helped her get specific about what success would actually look like.

"If we could design the ideal outcome," I asked, "what would that include?"

Her answer was more comprehensive than just loan forgiveness:

"I want to complete my PSLF requirements by working for a qualifying organization, but I don't want to get stuck there forever. Ideally, after I achieve loan forgiveness, I'd find a way back to my current organization, the one I love, but in a role that uses more of my capabilities and provides more influence over the outcomes I care about."

This precision was crucial because it revealed that the optimal solution wasn't just about completing loan forgiveness requirements but creating a strategic career path that would ultimately bring her back to where she wanted to be, but in an enhanced capacity.

A - Analyze: Identifying the Real Obstacles

The obvious obstacle was the organizational classification issue that created the loan forgiveness problem. But as we analyzed the situation more deeply, other barriers became visible:

Obstacle 1: Time pressure from political changes creates urgency that might lead to suboptimal decisions

Obstacle 2: Her current organization's inability to change its classification status

Obstacle 3: Limited awareness of alternative solutions beyond "stay forever or leave forever"

Obstacle 4: Assumption that leaving her current organization temporarily would mean permanently giving up her connection to work she loved

Obstacle 5: Belief that taking a transitional role for loan forgiveness purposes would derail her long-term career goals

Obstacle 6: Treating the PSLF completion and eventual return as separate challenges instead of phases of an integrated strategy

The most significant insight was that she was approaching this as a binary choice rather than a multi-phase strategic plan that could potentially achieve all her goals.

R - Reframe: Shifting Limiting Beliefs

Several limiting beliefs were constraining her thinking about possible solutions:

Old Belief: "I have to choose between loan forgiveness and doing work I love." **New Belief**: "I might be able to achieve both goals through strategic sequencing if I'm creative about the approach."

Old Belief: "Leaving my current organization means permanently giving up my career passion." **New Belief**: "A strategic departure could position me to return in an even better capacity."

Old Belief: "Taking a transitional job for loan forgiveness will derail my career trajectory." **New Belief**: "The right transitional role could actually enhance my capabilities and make me more valuable when I'm ready to return."

Old Belief: "I need to solve this quickly before the political situation changes." **New Belief**: "I can create a strategic plan that works across multiple timelines while building capabilities for the long term."

The most essential belief transformation was helping her see this situation as an opportunity to create her ultimate professional situation rather than just a crisis to survive.

I - Identify: Recognizing Hidden Resources

As we inventoried her available assets, several powerful resources became apparent:

Relationship Resources: She had built strong connections with leadership and colleagues at her current organization. These relationships had been developed over years of excellent work and genuine mutual respect.

Reputation Resources: She was highly regarded in her field and known for delivering exceptional results. This reputation would travel with her to any new organization.

Timing Resources: The political timeline, while compressed, still provided enough time to execute a strategic transition if planned systematically.

Knowledge Resources: Through her current position, she had gained insights into organizational management and strategic approaches that could be valuable anywhere she went.

Strategic Resources: She understood her industry's landscape, key players, and organizational cultures, which positioned her to choose transitional opportunities strategically.

Network Resources: Her industry connections included leaders at various qualifying organizations who knew her work quality and could provide opportunities.

Financial Resources: Her current salary provided stability during the transition period, and we had savings to support any temporary adjustments.

Most importantly, she demonstrated the capability for high-level strategic thinking and execution that could justify enhanced roles at her current or potential transitional organizations.

T - Take Action: Developing the Strategic Plan

Based on our analysis, we developed a multi-phase approach that was both creative and systematic:

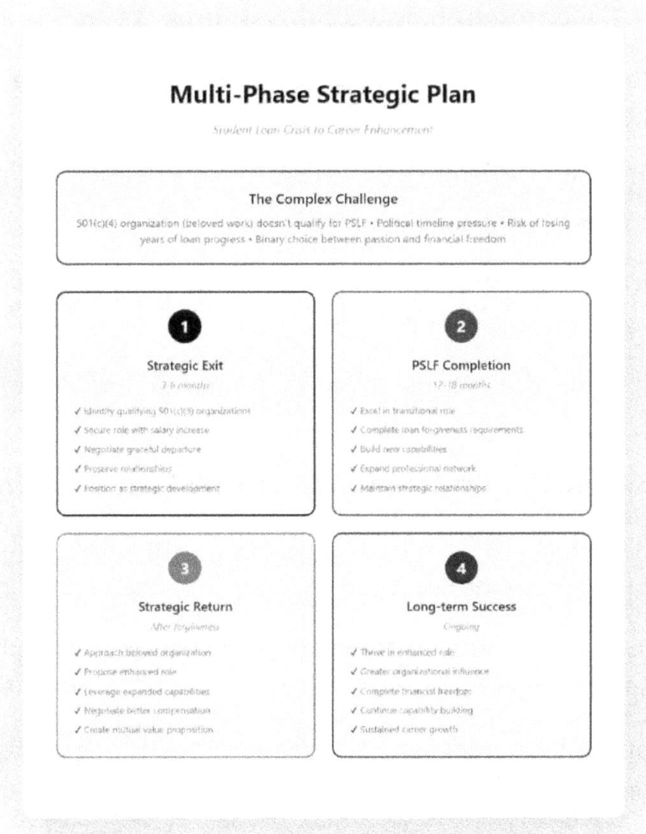

Phase 1: Strategic Exit and Transition (3-6 months)

- Identify qualifying 501(c)(3) organizations with roles that aligned with her career trajectory and offered salary increases

- Negotiate departure from the current beloved organization in a way that preserves relationships and leaves doors open

- Secure transitional role that not only qualified for PSLF but also enhanced her capabilities and market value

- Position the move as strategic professional development rather than a permanent departure

Phase 2: PSLF Completion and Skill Building (12-18 months)

- Excel in the transitional role while completing loan forgiveness requirements

- Build new capabilities, expand professional network, and demonstrate enhanced expertise

- Maintain strategic relationships with previous organizations through industry connections

- Document achievements and expanded skill set for future positioning

Phase 3: Strategic Return Negotiation (After loan forgiveness)

- After achieving loan forgiveness, approach the previous organization about returning

- Propose a new role that leverages expanded capabilities gained during the transition

- Negotiate an enhanced position with greater influence, responsibility, and higher compensation

- Create a value proposition that makes her return beneficial for the organization

Phase 4: Long-term Success Optimization

- Thrive in an enhanced role at a beloved organization with financial freedom

- Continue building on expanded capabilities and network

- Contribute to organizational success while pursuing personal fulfillment

- Use the experience as a foundation for continued career growth

The key insight was that instead of seeing the loan forgiveness requirement as forcing her away from her ideal work, we could use it as an opportunity to build capabilities that would make her even more valuable when she returned.

Y - Yield: Building Sustainable Momentum

The plan included elements designed to create lasting value rather than just solving the immediate crisis:

- Each phase would build capabilities and relationships that enhanced her long-term career prospects

- Success in transitional roles would demonstrate her adaptability and strategic thinking

- The approach would strengthen her reputation across multiple organizations in her field

- The experience would provide confidence and frameworks for handling future complex challenges

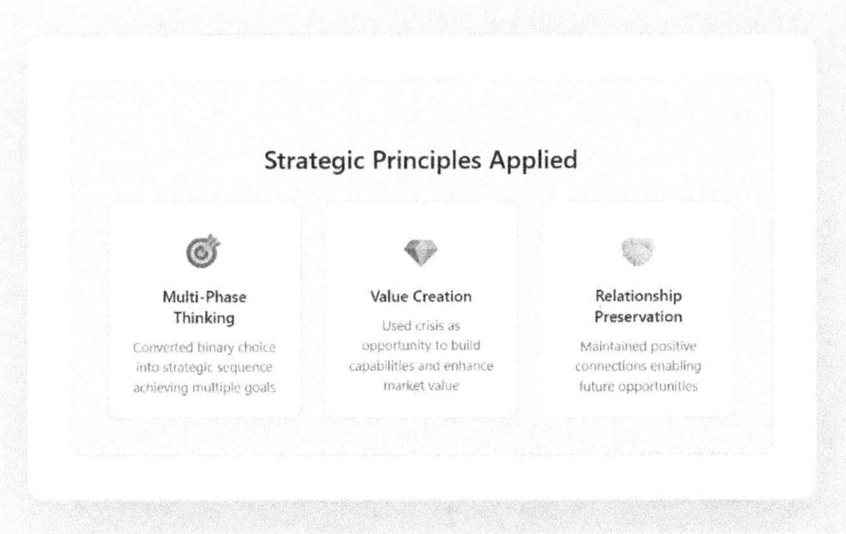

The Execution and Results

The plan unfolded systematically across multiple phases, with even better outcomes than we had initially envisioned:

Phase 1 Success: She successfully identified and transitioned to a qualifying 501(c)(3) organization in a role that met PSLF requirements, paid a significantly higher salary, and expanded her skill set in strategic areas. She left her beloved organization on excellent terms, with leaders understanding this was a strategic financial decision and expressing hope that she might return someday.

Phase 2 Success: While completing her loan forgiveness requirements, she excelled in her transitional role, building new capabilities in areas like strategic planning and organizational development. Her work gained recognition both within her new organization and across the industry. After 14 months in this role, she received full loan forgiveness through the PSLF program, eliminating our substantial student debt burden.

Phase 3 Success: With her student loans forgiven and expanded capabilities demonstrated, she approached her original organization about returning. By this time, her former boss was planning retirement, creating opportunities for organizational restructuring. Using insights from her transitional experience, she proposed a newly created leadership role that would oversee multiple departments and address emerging organizational gaps. The organization enthusiastically welcomed her back with a substantial salary increase that exceeded even her transitional role and significantly more influence over the outcomes she cared most about.

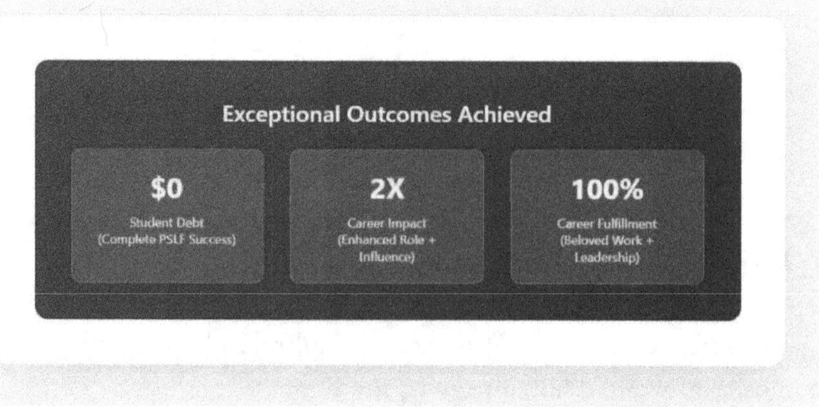

Unexpected Bonus: About nine months after leaving her organization, the federal government allowed a special exemption that made her original organization retroactively eligible for PSLF. If she had stayed, she would have qualified anyway, but by then she was thriving in her new role while making plans to return to a much higher salary, expanded capabilities, and greater impact than she'd ever had before.

The Method Validation

What made this experience so significant for validating The CLARITY Code™ wasn't just that it worked; it was how comprehensively it worked across multiple complex variables:

Systematic Rather Than Random: Instead of jumping between different solutions or making decisions based on immediate emotions, the method provided a framework for analyzing the situation comprehensively and developing strategic responses that addressed all key factors.

Creative Rather Than Obvious: The obvious solutions were either unsatisfactory (stay and lose loan progress) or suboptimal (leave for any qualifying organization and hope for the best). The method helped us identify a creative alternative that was better than either obvious option.

Multi-Phase Rather Than Short-Term: Instead of just solving the immediate loan crisis, the approach created a strategic career trajectory that achieved multiple goals across an extended timeline.

Relationship-Based Rather Than Transactional: The approach leveraged and strengthened existing relationships while creating value for multiple organizations rather than just seeking individual benefit.

Opportunity-Focused Rather Than Problem-Focused: Instead of just trying to escape a bad situation, the method helped create a better situation than she'd had before the crisis emerged.

Sustainable Rather Than Temporary: The solution didn't just solve the immediate loan forgiveness challenge—it positioned her for continued growth and impact in work she genuinely loved, with financial freedom and enhanced capabilities.

The Unconscious Competence Realization

Perhaps most importantly, this experience demonstrated that The CLARITY Code™ worked even when applied unconsciously by someone who had internalized its principles.

I hadn't formally told my wife about the framework or walked her through each step. I had simply applied the systematic thinking I'd developed, and it had guided our conversation naturally through each element needed for comprehensive problem-solving.

This suggested that the method wasn't just a useful tool for conscious application, it was a way of thinking about challenges that could become intuitive for anyone who practiced it consistently.

The Meta-Learning

Beyond solving my wife's specific situation, this experience taught me several crucial lessons about the broader applications of The CLARITY Code™:

Complex Challenges Require Systematic Approaches: The more interconnected and time-sensitive the challenge, the more important it becomes to work through each step thoroughly rather than jumping to quick solutions.

Multi-Phase Thinking Reveals Superior Solutions: Many situations that seem like binary choices actually offer creative third alternatives that achieve multiple goals through strategic sequencing.

Strategic Patience Often Beats Urgent Action: Taking time to develop comprehensive plans often leads to better outcomes than reacting quickly to immediate pressures.

Capability Building Can Be Integrated into Problem Solving: Challenges that seem like obstacles can become opportunities for development if approached strategically.

Stakeholder Value Creation Multiplies Options: Solutions that create value for multiple parties are more likely to be embraced and supported than solutions that only serve one person's interests.

Relationship Preservation Enables Future Opportunities: Maintaining positive relationships during difficult transitions often creates possibilities that aren't visible in the immediate term.

But the most profound realization was that the method had become more than just a problem-solving framework—it had become a way of approaching life's challenges with confidence, creativity, and systematic thinking that could handle even the most complex multi-variable situations.

My wife's crisis could have been a source of stress, financial pressure, and career compromise. Instead, it became an opportunity to create her ideal professional situation while achieving complete financial freedom from student debt, strengthening relationships across multiple organizations, and demonstrating capabilities that opened doors for future opportunities.

That's the ultimate validation of any methodology: not just that it works, but it transforms how you see and responds to challenges permanently, enabling you to create outcomes better than what seemed possible when the challenge first emerged.

The CLARITY Code™ had passed its most important test. It was time to share it with others who might need this kind of systematic approach to transforming complexity into clarity in their lives.

CHAPTER 16
YOUR CLARITY REVOLUTION

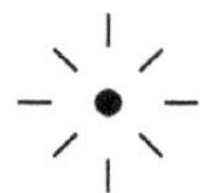

"When you learn to systematically transform complexity into clarity, what looked impossible begins to look inevitable." ©

The methodology that saved my career and transformed my wife's path wasn't meant to stay private.

As I sit here writing this final chapter, I'm struck by how far this journey has taken us—from that sterile conference room where I first realized I was stuck, through the late-night spreadsheet analysis that revealed my natural talents, to the systematic development of a framework that has helped countless people navigate their own complex challenges.

But this book isn't really about my story or my wife's success. It's about the recognition that every person who feels stuck, trapped, or unable to move forward already possesses the raw materials needed for transformation. They just need a systematic way to confront their reality, locate their destination, analyze their obstacles, reframe their thinking, identify their resources, take strategic action, and yield sustainable momentum.

What started as a personal survival strategy has become something much larger: a repeatable method for turning any stuck point into a breakthrough opportunity.

Now it's your turn to join this revolution; not the kind that tears things down, but the kind that builds people up by showing them what's possible when they learn to navigate complexity with confidence and creativity.

Why This Matters Now More Than Ever

We live in an era of unprecedented complexity and change. The career paths that worked for previous generations no longer exist. The social and economic systems that once provided stability are shifting rapidly. The personal and professional challenges people face require skills that most of us were never taught in school.

Yet despite having access to more information, opportunities, and resources than any generation in history, millions of people feel more stuck than ever. They feel trapped in unfulfilling careers, constrained by financial pressures, overwhelmed by relationship challenges, and paralyzed by the gap between their current reality and their dreams.

The problem isn't a lack of options; it's a lack of a systematic approach for navigating complex situations where multiple variables intersect in confusing ways. Most people either:

- Jump between random solutions without strategic thinking

- Get paralyzed by analysis without taking systematic action

- Focus on obvious obstacles while missing deeper systemic issues

- Try to change external circumstances without addressing internal barriers

- Create short-term fixes without building long-term capabilities

The CLARITY Code™ provides an alternative: a comprehensive framework for approaching any challenge with the same systematic thinking that successful people naturally use, but that most people have never learned explicitly.

What Makes This Method Different

Having studied and applied countless personal development approaches over the years, I can tell you that most of them fall into one of several categories:

Motivational approaches that inspire you to think positively but don't provide practical frameworks for handling complex challenges.

Tactical approaches that give you specific strategies but don't help you think systematically about which strategies to use when.

Psychological approaches that help you understand your inner barriers, but don't bridge to external action and results.

Strategic approaches that teach business thinking but don't address the personal and emotional aspects of being stuck.

The CLARITY Code™ integrates the best elements of all these approaches into a single, systematic process that works whether you're dealing with career challenges, relationship issues, financial pressures, creative blocks, or any other complex life situation.

More importantly, it's based on principles that I discovered through necessity rather than theory. Every element of the method has been tested in real situations with real stakes, refined through actual practice, and validated through helping others achieve tangible results.

This isn't academic theory; it's practical methodology that works in the messy, complicated, time-pressured world where most of us actually live.

The Difference Between Stuck and Strategic

The fundamental insight that drives The CLARITY Code™ is this: **The difference between people who stay stuck and people who break through isn't talent, luck, or favorable circumstances. It's the willingness to approach complexity with systematic clarity rather than random hope.**

Every person who is thriving today once faced situations that felt impossible. The difference between breakthrough and breakdown isn't the absence of challenges; it's the presence of systematic approaches for transforming complexity into clarity, confusion into direction, and obstacles into opportunities.

When you learn to systematically transform complexity into clarity, what looked impossible begins to look inevitable.

Your Journey Starts with a Single Step

If you've read this far, you're probably feeling some combination of inspiration and overwhelm. The stories and frameworks make sense intellectually, but applying them to your situation might feel daunting.

That's completely normal. Every person I've ever helped through The CLARITY Code™ process has felt exactly the same way at the beginning.

The key is to start where you are, with what you have, facing whatever challenge is most pressing in your life right now. You don't need to master the entire method before you begin—you just need to be willing to apply it one step at a time to your actual situation.

Here's how to begin:

Step 1: Choose Your Challenge

Identify one area of your life where you feel most stuck right now. Don't try to address everything at once. Pick the situation that either:

- Is it causing you the most stress or frustration daily

- Would create the most positive ripple effects if improved

- Feels most urgent due to external deadlines or pressures

- Represents the biggest gap between your current reality and what you want

Step 2: Commit to the Complete Process

The CLARITY Code™ works as an integrated system. Skipping steps or jumping around will significantly reduce its effectiveness. Commit to systematically working through all seven letters, even if some steps feel unnecessary or uncomfortable.

Give yourself permission to spend real time on this process. Most life-changing insights don't come from quick fixes. They come from thorough analysis and strategic thinking applied consistently over time.

Step 3: Start with Systematic Self-Assessment

Begin with the C—Confront your current reality. This means being brutally honest about where you actually are versus where you think you are or wish to be.

While this book has shown you the power of clear seeing through stories and examples, transformation happens through application, not just understanding. That's why I've created The CLARITY Code™ Workbook—a comprehensive implementation guide with specific reality assessment exercises, structured reflection questions, and systematic tools designed to cut through the stories and justifications that usually cloud clear thinking.

The workbook takes you step-by-step through the exact process of confronting your current reality, with exercises that have been refined through helping many people see their situations with the clarity needed for a breakthrough.

Step 4: Apply Each Step Systematically

Work through each letter of The CLARITY Code™ using the detailed processes and frameworks I've developed specifically for implementation.

The workbook provides the structured exercises, worksheets, and step-by-step guidance that turn the concepts you've learned into concrete progress on your specific challenges.

However, knowing what to do and successfully navigating the inevitable resistance and complexity that arise during real transformation are two different things. That's why I've also developed The CLARITY Navigator—a companion guide that provides the deeper insights, alternative perspectives, and coaching guidance you need exactly when you need it most.

The Navigator anticipates your questions, helps you work through the resistance that emerges at each step, and provides the kind of breakthrough insights that typically only come from one-on-one coaching. Together, these tools give you everything necessary to move from feeling stuck to creating the breakthrough you're seeking.

Step 5: Expect Resistance and Work Through It

Every step of the method will trigger some form of internal resistance. Your mind will try to convince you to skip difficult exercises, settle for vague answers, or jump ahead to action without completing the analysis.

This resistance is normal and actually indicates that you're approaching something important. The Navigator provides specific guidance for working through resistance at each step rather than avoiding it, helping you push through the discomfort that often precedes a breakthrough.

Step 6: Build on Small Wins

As you begin taking action based on your CLARITY analysis, celebrate progress and use each small success as evidence that the method works and that you're capable of handling your challenge effectively.

These early wins build the confidence needed for tackling more complex aspects of your situation.

Step 7: Share Your Journey

Find ways to share what you're learning with others who might benefit. Teaching the method reinforces your own understanding and creates accountability for continued application.

You don't need to be an expert to help others; you just need to be one step ahead and willing to share what you've discovered.

The Ripple Effects You Can Expect

While each person's journey through The CLARITY Code™ is unique, most people experience several common transformations that extend far beyond solving their original challenge:

Increased Confidence in Handling Complexity

Once you've successfully navigated one complex challenge using systematic thinking, you approach future difficulties with much greater confidence. You know you have a framework that works, regardless of the specific content of the challenge.

Enhanced Problem-Solving Capabilities

The method teaches you to think strategically about any situation involving multiple variables, conflicting interests, or unclear solutions. This capability serves you throughout your personal and professional life.

Improved Relationship Building

Understanding how to create value for others while pursuing your own goals dramatically improves your ability to build productive relationships in any context.

Greater Comfort with Uncertainty

Instead of needing perfect information before taking action, you become comfortable developing strategies that can adapt as new information becomes available.

Stronger Sense of Personal Agency

Rather than feeling like circumstances control your life, you develop confidence that you can influence outcomes through strategic thinking and systematic action.

Expanded Definition of What's Possible

Successfully creating outcomes that initially seemed impossible changes your beliefs about what's achievable in other areas of your life.

The Choice That Changes Everything

At this point, you have a choice that will determine whether this book becomes just another interesting read or the beginning of a fundamental shift in how you approach life's challenges.

You can set this book aside, return to your normal routine, and hope your stuck points resolve through time or luck. Many people make this choice, and there's nothing wrong with it. Some challenges are resolved naturally, and not everyone needs to become a systematic problem-solver.

Or you can decide to join the growing number of people who refuse to accept being stuck as a permanent condition. You can apply these frameworks to your situation, work through the resistance and discomfort that comes with honest self-assessment, and systematically create the changes you want to see in your life.

This choice isn't about optimism or pessimism—it's about agency. It's about recognizing that while you can't control everything that happens to you, you can control how systematically and strategically you respond to whatever challenges arise.

The Movement Grows Through Individual Action

The CLARITY revolution doesn't happen through grand gestures or public campaigns. It happens one person at a time, as individuals decide to take responsibility for navigating their challenges systematically rather than hoping for external rescue.

Every time someone applies this method to gain clarity, they become more confident in their ability to handle complexity. That confidence radiates outward, inspiring others to believe that transformation is possible for them too.

Whenever someone shares what they've learned through the process, they help others see new possibilities for their situations.

Every time someone uses these frameworks to create value for others while pursuing their own goals, they demonstrate that success doesn't require taking advantage of others or succeeding at someone else's expense.

This is how positive change spreads—not through force or persuasion, but through example and invitation.

Your Clarity Future Starts Now

As I finish writing this book, I'm filled with excitement about what you might create once you begin applying these ideas to your own life. I can't predict what specific challenges you'll face or what particular outcomes you'll achieve, but I can predict this:

If you systematically apply The CLARITY Code™ to your real situation, you will discover capabilities you didn't know you had. You will see possibilities that weren't visible before you began. You will create results that seemed impossible when you first felt stuck.

More importantly, you will develop an unshakeable confidence that no challenge is too complex to navigate, no situation is truly hopeless, and no goal is impossible if you're willing to think strategically and act systematically.

That confidence will serve you for the rest of your life, in ways you can't yet imagine.

The Invitation

The frameworks are ready. The implementation tools are available. The only remaining question is whether you're ready to discover what becomes possible when you stop accepting being stuck as a permanent condition and start treating it as a temporary challenge that can be systematically addressed.

Remember this: complexity isn't the enemy—confusion is. When you learn to systematically transform complexity into clarity, what looked impossible begins to look inevitable.

Your impossible situation is waiting to become your greatest opportunity.

The code is clarity. The method is systematic. The results are inevitable.

The journey continues...

ABOUT THE AUTHOR

Jeremy Scott is a strategic consultant and the creator of The CLARITY Code™, a systematic methodology for transforming complex challenges into breakthrough opportunities. With nearly two decades of experience in healthcare strategy and business consulting, Jeremy has helped professionals and organizations navigate their most challenging situations with confidence and clarity.

After earning his MBA while working full-time and joining a Big Four consulting firm, Jeremy discovered firsthand how traditional problem-solving approaches often fail when facing complex, multi-variable challenges. His experience being systematically sabotaged in a toxic corporate environment became the crucible for developing The CLARITY Code™, a framework that has since helped countless individuals move from feeling stuck to creating strategic momentum in their careers and lives.

Jeremy's approach combines analytical rigor with practical wisdom, drawing from his background in healthcare and life sciences operations, business strategy, and organizational dynamics. He believes that every person possesses the resources needed for transformation; they just need a systematic way to see and leverage them.

When he's not helping others gain clarity on their challenges, Jeremy enjoys traveling, mixing music, cooking new recipes, spending time with his family, being active in various organizations, and finding humor in literally everything. He has always had a curious mindset and an affinity for figuring out how other people's minds work and what shaped their lives. He hails from the great state of Georgia but lives with his family in the Washington, D.C. metro area.

www.htjstrategiesandsolutions.com

ACKNOWLEDGMENTS

This book exists because of the people who believed in both the methodology and the messenger long before either was fully formed.

To Jah: You are my inspiration, my leader, and my rock. You inspire me each day and keep me grounded and balanced. I would be nowhere without you.

To my wife: You didn't just support this journey, you became its most important validation. Watching you apply The CLARITY Code™ to transform what seemed impossible into your ideal career outcome proved that this methodology works even when applied unconsciously. Your willingness to let me share our story, including the vulnerable moments, makes this book authentic rather than theoretical.

To my daughter: You are very young right now, but ultimately, you will realize that you have motivated me and blessed me so much more than words can say. Hopefully, you take this guidance and apply it to your life someday.

To my parents: You instilled the deep-seated principles that became the foundation for everything I've accomplished. Your unwavering support and belief in me made this journey possible.

To my brothers and sisters: Thank you for keeping me grounded, pushing me to be better, and putting up with my constant need to analyze everything. Your honest feedback and unconditional love have shaped who I am today.

To my sister-in-law: Thank you for helping me mindmap my ideas and convincing me to actually write this book.

To my colleagues and mentors in consulting: Especially those who showed me how complex systems really work versus how they're supposed to work. Your willingness to share the unwritten rules and informal dynamics taught me that understanding the game being played is often more important than playing it harder. Special thanks to Dr. Pratt, whose question, "Do you realize you just described a methodology?" changed how I thought about my natural problem-solving approach.

To Marcus, David, and the others (names changed to protect privacy): Who trusted me enough to let me guide them through their stuck points before I had any formal framework. Your willingness to be vulnerable about your challenges and systematic about finding solutions helped me understand that this wasn't just personal intuition but a replicable process. Thank you for letting me share your stories and for becoming living proof that The CLARITY Code™ works.

To Leroy, Maurice, and Roderick: Who read rough drafts, completed early versions of exercises, and provided honest feedback about what worked and what didn't. Your input helped refine every element of this methodology.

To my various colleagues: Who taught me that the most valuable skills often feel natural to you but difficult for others. Your questions about how I approached complex situations forced me to reverse-engineer my own thinking and discover the patterns that became this framework.

To everyone who has ever felt systematically stuck: Your experiences validate why this book needed to exist. Complex challenges require systematic solutions, not just harder effort or positive thinking. I hope The CLARITY Code™ gives you the same confidence it gave me: that no situation is truly impossible when you learn to see it clearly and respond strategically.

Finally, to anyone who takes these ideas and applies them to their own situation: You are the real test of whether this methodology has value. The framework only works when it's applied systematically to real challenges by real people. Thank you in advance for proving that transformation is possible when complexity is converted into clarity.